Chasing Success,

Finding Purpose

The Dontonio Wingfield Story

By Dontonio B. Wingfield

Dedicated to my children -

Ashley
Brianna ("Lips")
Dequan
Dontonio Jr.
Jay
Autumn ("Butterfly")
Donovan ("Dono")
London
Donjuwan

And to all my grandchildren

I never gave up on becoming better.

With Gratitude . . .

I thank God for never leaving my side.

I am grateful for my mom and dad, my brothers and the rest of my family, including my grandmothers, uncles, aunties and cousins.

So many people have been there for me at different times of my life, including Coach Willie Boston, Coach Bob Huggins, Mrs. Gaynelle Johnson, Ms. Hannah Hudson, all of my godsisters, godbrothers, godnieces and godnephews.

I am grateful for all my homies who know the real me.

Thanks to the City of Albany. I have always wanted to represent you to the fullest.

Thanks to the University of Cincinnati.

Thanks to Westover High School.

Thanks to Bo and Bonny Dorough and family, Jay Sharpe, Darrel Finnicum, Lisa Kendrick, Jason Spears, Mr. Postell, Bruce Pittman, The Nix family, Corey Chaney and family, Bob Beauchamp, Carlton Fletcher, Jesse Smith and family, Trey Underwood and family, and
Curtis Marshall.

Table of Contents

Foreword

Amazingly profound is the term that depicts the volume of work you hold in your hands. The journey that awaits you inside these pages describes trials that can only be compared with the humility Don employs and demonstrates today to overcome the mountains he has come face to face with.

The content following epitomizes the very essence of life - a series of choices. The grace that bestows this vessel and his life is transcendent beyond his God-given athleticism. That cup has run over and has infected and affected lives from yesteryear, yesterday, today and moving forward. Anyone familiar with the game knows Dontonio Wingfield.

Many a soul will respond to this tremendously transparent work with a judgmental eye. However, the same grace God uses to overcome our challenges is the same grace He used to posture Don to unabashedly share his life story in this book, which (not unlike ours) is still a work in progress. Don lived this life and sheds the facades, and myths and clears the blurred lines for us all. Get ready for a compelling and eye opening ride!

> *"For by grace you have been saved through faith,*
> *and that not of yourselves;*
> *it is the gift of God, not of works, lest anyone should boast."*
> (Ephesians 2:8-9, nkjv)

William (Bill) Caldwell
Pastor and Founder - Life Changing Christian Church
Albany, GA

Introduction

Finding your purpose is what defines your greatness.

Those words have become the story of my life. As a young man growing up in a small town, I believed greatness had to do with things like money, fame and girls. I thought success was determined by one's athletic abilities. But I have been to the highest level of basketball competition in the world and found out those qualities were all cheap imitations of greatness. Along my journey I learned greatness goes much deeper. Greatness is a life lived with purpose. Greatness rises up from individuals who know why they are on earth. That kind of greatness is what drives me these days. I wake up each morning with great peace because I am doing what I was made to do. I am making an impact that will long outlive me because I am making a positive difference in the world of young people.

I share my story to inspire my readers to discover their purpose in life and to live out that purpose with passion. Purpose leads to true greatness, the kind that values others and seeks to serve people. That's the greatness that comes from within.

I hope to pass along to younger generations the wisdom I have gained from my life. I made some bad choices early on that led me to some painful situations. I learned from those mistakes. As a result, I want to help young men and women make wiser decisions and avoid the kinds of consequences that can last a lifetime.

This is my story, the good and the bad, the right and the wrong. It is all laid out before you as honestly and accurately as I know how. I own all that is mine. Writing this book has been a long and difficult journey, but it has been worth every minute knowing I am helping others. I hope you will pass my book along to others who need to read my story and find wisdom and encouragement as they face similar challenges along this journey of life.

Becoming Somebody

Chapter 1

In the early days, my home life was good. My parents were together, and my dad was working a great job at a pest control company. I remember we had a brown, four-door Buick that he kept clean and shiny. I still remember those happier times when we lived in our own home as a family. We were together and it felt good. However, behind the scenes of my happy family was a simmering pot of addiction that would eventually boil over and bring those good days to an end.

My father was a functioning alcoholic. He was a hard worker who showed up for work every morning and did a great job while there. Then he would come home each evening and get drunk. He was drunk on the weekends, too. He also began smoking weed with his friend, Buddy. I can still recall the two of them in the living room on the sofa, and in front of them on a small table would be Tops papers, matches, beer and a small manilla envelope of marijuana. I would walk through the room going outside to play. I can still remember smelling the stuff.

Before long, the habit became greater than my dad. He was hooked and there was no going back. That is when our happy lives turned to anger, fighting, hardships, and fear. His addictions began to show up everywhere, including home and work. He and my mom argued all the time. Looking back, I don't remember a time when he did not fuss at her. I recall many nights lying in the bed listening to them holler at each other. It is something I have never gotten over. The noises from their arguments haunt me to this day. I have never slept in the dark or in the silence. The television in my bedroom is never turned off. It is on day and night.

My dad abused my mom physically and verbally. Their fights were terrible. But to their credit, they did try to work things out. My father went to rehab on several occasions trying to kick his habit. I remember him being gone for stretches of time and then he would show up clean and neat. It would be all good for a short time, and then he would somehow get caught up in the alcohol and it would go downhill again. We would find bottles of gin and vodka hidden all over the house. Mom gave him lots of chances to get clean. It was a back-and-forth relationship for a couple of years, but the addictions proved to be too much. They finally split up for good. He lost his job and even though my mom worked as a hostess at a local country club, we lost our car and house. We had to move in with my grandmother in an area called Washington Homes. It was about this time my younger brother, Shelt, was born.

My father was also abusive to the rest of the family. One incident sticks out in my mind. One morning I had ironed a shirt for myself and I left the iron out. My little brother was rolling around in his walker, and he hit the ironing board and knocked the iron over. The hot water spilled out on him and burned his chest severely. Everyone was upset and mad at me. My dad slapped the hell out of me for that mistake. That was the way it was around our house. My father ruled over us all.

Yet even after all of that, my dad was still special to me. Even though he made some poor decisions, I looked up to him. After he and my mother split up for good, she would take me to his house on the weekends. My brothers did not want to go, but I always did. My older brother was busy with basketball. My younger brother did not really know him. Part of the reason I wanted to visit him was because he made me feel special when no one else did. When I went with him and was around others, he would always speak highly of me. He would tell others that I was going to be a football star. He also taught me how to drive at an early age. I thought that was cool because none of my other 11-year-old friends were driving. Since I was big for my age, the cops never thought I was underage. The main place I drove him was to the liquor store, of course. His motives did not bother me. All that mattered to me was that I got to drive.

It was my dad who also got me started in sports. My first experience was not on the basketball court. It was on the football field. My father wanted me to play football. When I was about 8, he took me to the tryouts for the Green Machines! He told the coach I would be a great quarterback. The only problem was that I had never played football, much less quarterback. All I knew was that if you had the ball, you couldn't let anyone tackle you. I didn't even know the fundamentals of the game. I had no idea what to do so, when the ball was snapped, I did the only thing I knew to do. I ran! Everyone laughed at me. Football fell through.

Perhaps my father's greatest impressions on me as a child had to do with lessons I would take into adulthood. For instance, my father taught me how to be tough. He told me not to let anyone put their hands on me without consequences. I interpreted his lessons of toughness to go all in if someone started a fight with me. My father also taught me how to treat a lady. I remember seeing him with women besides my mother, not realizing what was actually going on. But this was how I thought a husband and dad was supposed to be. That's how many of the older men in my surroundings treated women too. I know my father was not always aware of me learning from his example. Alcohol changed him. I understand now this was where I got my addictive personality.

Chapter 2

The only stability I had during these early years was my grandmother, Grandma Bell. We always ran to her when things got out of hand. She had a small, two-bedroom apartment in the Washington Homes, a government housing project. The apartment complex was all brick, concrete and cinder blocks. Her apartment was tight when we all stayed there. We boys would sleep on the floor, and my mom would sleep in the spare bedroom with our younger brother. My grandmother kept a very clean house. It was immaculate. Children were not allowed to sit on the sofa. We either sat on the floor or went outside. Of course, housekeeping was her profession. She was a maid for a man named Mr. Shackleford. He lived in a very large house. In fact, it looked like a mansion to us. She would take the bus every day to work for him. I learned a lot from her about keeping clean and cooking. She also taught me to keep a peppermint in my pocket. My memories of Grandmother include her love for Pepsi colas and her delicious fried chicken. She also had an air conditioner in the window. Most people back then did not have air conditioning, but she did. She was a bit stingy with it, but when she did turn it on, we would sit in front of it and the cold air felt so good. Most of all, I remember her being there for us when life was hard. For a little boy in an unsettled home like mine, a safe place like my grandmother's home meant everything.

Eventually we were able to move out from my grandmother's apartment to our own place in Willowood Apartments a couple of miles from her. Although it was similar to the housing projects where my grandmother lived, it was almost a different world for me. One of the main differences was the friends I had. When we lived with my grandmother, none of my friends played basketball. We just hung out together, riding bikes and playing all kinds of games outside. We even used to do flips. Those early childhood games helped me develop my coordination. When I wanted to play ball, I went to the Cedar Street Boys Club. However, moving to Willowood allowed me to live closer to Henderson Gym, where all of my friends played basketball. In fact, that's all we did.

By this time, my older brother was becoming a well-known basketball player at Southside Middle School. When he went to Monroe High School he was a superstar. His name was Banastrues, but everyone knew him as B-Nasty. People thought of him as a celebrity. He got all of the attention. He always had girls around him. He had nice clothes. He had lots of friends. All of that made me jealous of him and motivated me to try to outdo him. I kept telling myself that one day I would outshine B-Nasty.

Not only was my brother a great basketball player, he was also a good guy, the very opposite of me. He was tall, handsome, and well-liked. People enjoyed being around him. He was my biggest influence on playing sports. He set the bar for me. He never got in trouble at school or home. I remember many times I would try to fight him and instead of him hitting me back, he would put me on the ground and pin my arms down so I would stop trying to hit him. He would not hit me back. But one time, I went too far. It was right before a championship basketball game that I got so angry at him I reached down and picked up a glass candy dish. Before I knew it, I threw it at his head and I hit my target. It cut him badly. Blood was everywhere. I remember watching him play that night in the game with a huge bandage wrapped around his head. At the time, it didn't bother me what I had done. But even now whenever I talk with him, I think about it and feel badly that he had to play in front of all those people in a region finals game with a big bandage wrapped around his head. B-Nasty has never brought it up to me. To him, it's like it never happened. That's how good of a man he was and still is. He always made me feel important. I looked up to him and he looked out for me. He never ignored me as his younger brother. He gave me attention. Even though I was jealous of him, I was proud to be B-Nasty's little brother.

Chapter 3

Teachers were surprised when I showed up at Southside Middle School. They thought they were getting another nice guy like B-Nasty. After all, I was his little brother. But they got just the opposite. They got the nasty version of B-Nasty. My mom worked frequently at night, so we were on our own mostly. Washington Homes and Willowood were rough places to live, so I fought a lot. I never backed down from anyone like my father had told me. I was determined that no one would bully me.

My family continued to struggle as well during my middle school years. We had moved out on our own and then had to move back in with my grandmother only to eventually move back out on our own. These moves put me in different school districts meaning I had to change schools each time. I attended Southside Middle School in the sixth and seventh grade, then

Radium Middle School in the seventh grade (second time) and then Southside in the eighth grade. This instability was a part of the reason I flunked the seventh grade and was not allowed to play basketball.

However, I could play at Henderson Gym, which was not far from our home in Willowood. The "No Pass, No Play" rule was not in effect at Henderson. It was on the other side of a wooded area. I remember walking down a path through those woods with my friends. We would cross a large drainage ditch and would regularly see foxes and snakes. The gym was "air conditioned" by large fans that sucked in air through the open doors. The blowing air felt more like a hair dryer. But that did not stop us from balling. We played basketball every day after school. The sneakers I wore were always too small, so my big toe would eventually poke a hole in those shoes. They also fed us free lunches called Billy Bo's. I have no idea where that name came from. Those days of hanging at the gym with my friends were the brightest moments of my childhood.

It was at Henderson Gym that I had my first coach who gave me some attention. Coach John Edwards was a big guy, so we nicknamed him Big John. He reminded us kids of the Incredible Hulk. He was not a yeller. He had a calm demeanor, which is one reason I liked him so much. Big John noticed me and my talent. He gave me a great deal of respect and believed in me. I respected him in return. He coached our recreation league teams during the school year.

During the summer, I participated in National Youth Sports Program, a program that combines fitness, fun, and learning. NYSP promotes self-respect and healthy living in mind, body and spirit. We played our games at our local college gym. More than 500 kids attended the games. That was what got us used to playing in front of loud and big crowds. Our team was always the best. I honestly don't remember us losing a game.

One of my teammates at NYSP was a kid named Melvin Drake. We called him "Poochie." He was outstanding and our team was awesome. We were mostly young middle school kids, and we would play high school junior varsity teams in the summer and beat them. I thought our team was great, but it still bothered me that Poochie got all the shine, just like my older brother had done. I got no shine, even though I knew I was better than he was. Poochie had made a name for himself around Albany as a basketball stud. Honestly, I think part of his fame was because of his curls. Poochie was a handsome guy with these big curls in his hair and all the girls liked him. Now I had no curls, but Poochie did. While I couldn't grow curls like Poochie, I could become a better ballplayer. So hearing his name motivated me to dream bigger and to work harder. I wanted a middle school championship. I wanted people to start talking about me and saying my name. Early on, I was beginning to think the name on the back of my jersey was what I should play for.

I met another guy named Antonio Leroy, a.k.a. "Stud." He lived next door to one of my favorite aunties, Janice. I would babysit my three little cousins, Josh, Jamaal and Sylvester ("Boobie") while she worked at night. He and I were alike in that both of us had a lot of potential as athletes. He excelled at football and I excelled at basketball. Both of us were very sure of ourselves and would always challenge each other. However, Stud was different than me in one major way - he was well-behaved. Teachers liked him. I often wondered how could he be so different while growing up with the same temptations I had. He did not smoke or drink alcohol. Looking back, I can see the main difference was that Stud's father was very involved in his life as well as his two brothers. His dad had weights and a weight bench on the front porch of their apartment and he worked out regularly with his sons. I remember working out with them one time, but I never went back because I did not have the work ethic. My dad never taught me about working hard. However, Stud's dad was supportive and gave him and his brothers a sense of stability. That was one thing I missed growing up. I still do.

Henderson Gym was where I began to make a name for myself playing basketball. I was bigger than the other kids and more athletic. I could shoot extremely well rarely missing open shots. I would go to different gyms to play and would dominate my age group. The league made me start playing on the older teams, and even then I would hold my own. I was able to dunk in middle school.

When I returned to Southside Middle School in the seventh grade, I had two special teachers who were a great help to me, Mrs. Bacon and Mr. Hubbard. The school assigned me to a special education class. It wasn't because I had any learning disabilities, it was because the smaller class size enabled me to focus better on my work. I couldn't pay attention in larger classes. I would goof off and cause problems so I was placed in special ed to help me stay focused. Mr. Hubbard was like a mentor to me at Southside. When he would talk to me, I would pay attention.

Chapter 4

Eighth grade was the year for me! I was back at Southside Middle School and was ready to follow in my big brother's footsteps and bring the city middle school basketball championship title to Southside. I wore his number that year, the number 12. It was a spectacular season. We beat every school we played, including Poochie's team. In fact, we beat them twice. I accomplished the goal I had set, winning the city middle school championship. And just as important to me was the fact that people were starting to say my name. They were talking about me.

The eighth grade was another memorable year because my brother was playing at Westover High School for Coach Willie Boston having transferred from Monroe High School, a rival high school. With my brother on the team, they had made it to the state championship game the previous year, but had lost against Griffin High School. Everyone was saying they would go far in the state playoffs, perhaps even win the whole thing. They did have a great season, but when they got to the tournament, Coach Boston and the Westover Patriots lost in the first round to Marist High School. I cried for him afterwards. I remember being in the locker room after the game promising the team that we would win the state title the next year. They looked at me like I was crazy!

While I was confident in my abilities on the basketball court, I was not so certain off the court. I was a teenager with many hangups who made some poor choices. I had a friend we called "Cooch." He and I would hang out together on the street corner getting drunk on Colt 45s, smoking weed and cigarettes. Smoking was nothing new to me. I remember lighting cigarettes for my mom and dad on the stove when I was a kid.

It was also about this time that girls and sex became a part of my life. I remember one specific young lady who grabbed my attention. It was at Southside Middle School when I saw her for the first time, and I thought she was the most beautiful girl in the world. I had never looked at girls before, but she grabbed my attention that day. However, she didn't know me at all. I was a kid with nothing. I was shy and self-conscious. I had nothing to offer her. But I told myself I would become a star one day like my brother and she would notice me then.

I have a lasting memory from those pre-teen years that impacted me into my adulthood. Since my mom worked at nights, my brothers and I were often at home by ourselves. My brother's popularity as a star athlete attracted the girls and lots of them. He would bring them home at night when my mom was gone. I recall sneaking out of my bedroom and lying on the floor watching him have sex with those girls. It was something I would never forget and it would shape the way I thought about being a star.

By the time I was in middle school, my dad was living in a trailer with a new family. Even though I would still go see him on the weekends, he never came to my ballgames and showed no interest in anything I was doing. When I spent the nights there, I could hear rats rambling around the kitchen. It was like an invasion. I was used to roaches, but rats were a different story.

His addictions had not disappeared. He was not living right, but I wanted to spend time with my dad. Although he had his problems, I had plenty of laughs with him. He was a funny man to me and one thing I knew was that when I went to his trailer, I wouldn't get yelled at. He might have been high most every weekend, but he never yelled at me like my mom. It was a sense of relief for me to visit him. She yelled at me a lot, but not my dad. I have never liked anyone yelling at me. I still don't.

My Grandmother

My Mom

My Dad

Middle School Championship Team

The Quad Squad

Chapter 5

By the summer of my ninth-grade year, I had grown to 6'7" and weighed more than 200 pounds. I was on a mission to make a name for myself, and I would not be stopped. That summer, Westover's summer league team was hot. We would beat other high schools by 40 points. We would score over a hundred at summer camp games. We called it "busting the clock." In those days, scoreboards had only two digit places for scores, so when we scored more than a hundred, we would "bust the clock." I made sure I led the team in scoring and rebounds and won numerous Most Valuable Player awards.

I walked in the first day of high school and I was excited, not only to begin high school, but to begin my career at Westover. Our upcoming basketball season was the talk around town. My big brother had just left for college, and now I was coming in to take his place. I was going to lead our team to the state championship. They had lost in the state championship game against Griffin High School two years before and then they lost in the first round his senior year against Marist High School. Our team believed we could win the state title, and we were excited to think it was within our reach.

My high school beginning was quite memorable. On the very first day of school, I was in the hallway between classes walking and talking with a friend. She and I had grown up together in the same neighborhood. We had not talked to each other since elementary school. Her boyfriend saw us talking and became quite jealous. He came up behind me and pushed me. I don't know what he expected, but fighting was a part of my upbringing. When he shoved me, all I could think about was what my dad had always told me, "If someone puts their hands on you, then you whip their ass!" He was not telling me to just defend myself; he was telling me to destroy the other person. I did exactly that. I instantly reacted, and I beat that guy badly. He never had a chance. It was a serious case of overreaction. I was much bigger than he was and I gave him all I had. I almost killed him. A teacher finally got through the ring of cheering students to pull me off of him. We both were suspended for 10 days.

News about the suspension traveled fast. Everyone in the Albany basketball world heard about it. Word on the street was that I was a hothead. I was finally getting all this attention I had been craving since I was a kid, but I was not liking it. One of the first lessons I learned was that being a star is not an easy life. It is hard having a target on your back. It feels like everyone is looking at you and wants something from you. High school was just the beginning.

Even though high school began with a fight and a suspension, I was still excited about being there. In a few short weeks, I knew I would be on the hardwood. That felt good. For as long as I can remember, the basketball court has been like a home to me. It has been the place I could be a part of a team that worked together, and I could be who I was made to be. I was ready for my freshman season to tip off. I would put on my brother's jersey, Number 12, and start for an Albany legend, Coach Willie Boston. It would be on from that point. It felt like the beginning of a new life.

I still remember our first game against a hometown rival, the Monroe High Tornadoes. Having grown up near the school, I knew a lot of people there and they knew me, too. I was excited to be playing in their famous gym. It was an incredible game. We beat the brakes off of Monroe. I was the highlight, scoring 30 points, getting 15 rebounds and having four thunderous dunks! It was the first of many great games I would have in high school.

This game was the moment I became a superhero to many people in Albany. Stardom had arrived for me. My dreams of getting the shine were coming true. Family and friends started saying I was better than my brother, and it felt good to hear that. I was no longer living in his shadow. Our season continued with success. Once again, Westover was in the state championship game. Our opponent was a crosstown rival, Albany High School.

That's right. The two best teams in Georgia were from the same town. I don't think that had ever happened. It was cool because I had friends at Albany High. Randy Cutts was their point guard. That afternoon he and I were swimming in the motel pool and when the coaches found us in the pool, they were all upset. Guess who else was on their team? Poochie. But this time he was without the curls. The game went down to the wire, but in the end we won, just as I had predicted the previous year. The Westover High Patriots reigned supreme in Georgia 3A high school basketball. Coach Boston got his first state championship. I was the Most Valuable Player and leading scorer. I became a high school All-American in my class. The news media were talking about me. College coaches from all over started calling. I was quickly becoming a mega superstar. What an awesome finish to my freshman year! As I look back on my high school days, I still think that first state championship team was the best. It was for me because I had older guys who gave leadership to the team. They put their arms around me and helped me. All I had to do was play. What mattered most to me was having the most points,

rebounds, dunks and girls.

Chapter 6

My fame brought greater prominence to my neighborhood. Willowood became the place to be in Albany because a majority of the Westover players was from there. I had a "squad" I began hanging with. It was made up of O.G.'s, older guys, in the neighborhood who gave me mostly what I wanted. They were hustlers for the most part. One of them was a guy named Vel. He was an outgoing guy. He had cars, girls and jewelry even in high school. We hung solid back in the day. He and I were in competition to see who could get the most girls. After I was awarded the Mr. Georgia title, he would always tell me I was the "Shit," which was a compliment. It was his way of saying I was "the man." My squad was like family to me. Many people would not understand this because most would look at them and think they were a bad influence on me. However, these guys actually protected me — from myself! They knew I had great potential to make it out of the neighborhood. But they also knew I could make some poor choices that could potentially and permanently keep me from going to the pros. They mentored me to make good choices, contrary to what everyone believed. They were not perfect, but they believed in me and wanted what was best for me. That's what family does. Even though they were hustlers, it was good to have people around.

Stardom was what I hoped it would be. I felt like I could do whatever I wanted. This was the success I had been dreaming of for a very long time. I had wealthy schoolmates who would pay me $20 for every dunk in games. I would intentionally try to dunk for the money. In my eyes, I had it all. The best part of it was the girls, girls, girls. They were everywhere offering me everything and, boy, did I indulge. I went from having sex only once in my life to having sex most every night. Since my mom worked at night, I was home by myself and I could do whatever I wanted. I was so tired from not sleeping, I wouldn't even go to school some days or I would skip school to hang out with girls who lived nearby. Once the basketball season was over, I forgot all about schoolwork. I was smoking and drinking all of the time. Life was like a party to me, but there was a down side to it as well.

Everyone loved me, or so I thought. My close circle of people tried to tell me otherwise. My coaches, godmothers, teammates and even my own mom would tell me that not everyone had my back. They said people had put a target on me, and they would do whatever they could to bring me down. And I thought to myself, "What!? I'm Dontonio. People like me. I'm a superstar. Nobody is out to get me." I was very naive. My innocence was crushed when I went to summer school after my freshman year.

Because I was living my dream, my grades bottomed out, and I had to attend summer term held at a rival school, Monroe High, the team we had beaten badly the previous year. One incident that turned ugly early in the term stands out in my mind.

I had made a smart remark to a teacher (who was a Westover teacher), and he sent me to the office. The principle decided the best way to handle me was to kick me out of summer school altogether. I felt like it was an overreaction. I believe he did it because of my status. He knew I would not be eligible to play in the fall term of my sophomore year if I missed summer school. The fact that the principle's son played on Monroe's basketball team made my support group of extended family question his decision to suspend me from summer school. This was an eye-opener to me that not everyone loved me. I had wanted stardom and I had gotten all of it, the good and the bad. I never knew it would be so hard. Coach Boston had tried to tell me about it. He had told me Albany had never seen anyone like me. I was different, and people would treat me differently. The incident at summer school made that very real. It also made me realize I could not trust everyone because not everyone was out to do me good. Some people actually wanted me to fail. That pill was hard to swallow for a 15-year-old kid.

However, I had many adults who truly believed in me and wanted me to succeed. They knew I was college material, and they wanted to help me get there. They would provide whatever my brother or I needed — food, clothes, money, shoes, or anything. For instance, Coach Boston was in my corner. We called him Coach B. He did more than just coach me. He would talk to me to help me understand. He was like a Moses to me, leading me to the promised land. He taught me lessons I am still practicing today. For instance, he taught me how to treat others as individuals. He was no "one size fits all" kind of coach. He understood every player was different and had to be treated differently. That lesson was not lost on me. When I work with kids today, I still work with them as individuals. He had a lasting impact on me and many others.

Mrs. Hannah Hudson was a long-time Westover fan. She taught at another high school, but all of her kids had gone to Westover and she was still a Patriots fan. She became a godmother to me. Mrs. Hudson would call me and talk to me about things that helped. She knew all of the team very well. I could do no wrong in her eyes. Over the years, Mrs. Hudson's children have continued to reach out to me. I still feel like a part of the Hudson family. She was a special person to me.

I had a math teacher who became a godmother to me, too, Mrs. Gaynelle Johnson. We called her Mrs. G. She was very understanding. She listened to me. I could talk to her. I took my math classes only from her. She was not a yeller. These people were very supportive. They gained my trust because I knew they were truly trying to help me. I knew I could depend on them.

Chapter 7

When my sophomore year started, I was determined to regain my eligibility so I studied hard while I was out because I wanted to play basketball. I needed to play basketball! However, I was also having sex most nights. By my sophomore year, girls were wanting time with me, the mega superstar of Albany. To me, I was becoming a living legend. I was full of myself! My home phone was ringing constantly, and my pager was always buzzing. By the end of my sophomore year, I had two kids on the way by two different girls, both from the Willowood neighborhood. I didn't want any kind of long-term relationship with either of the girls or with any girl, but I made a promise to them that I would always take care of them and the children. For a 16-year-old boy, it was all about the sex. Yet looking back, I remembered how much I enjoyed talking with them. I felt like I could share myself with the girls. I needed them to listen to me and they did. More than the sex, it was the sense of intimacy I had with them. The close connection with girls drew me in.

The season tipped off in the fall, and I could only watch because of my ineligibility. It was hurtful watching from the bench. It was also embarrassing. The team lost a couple of games that we would have won if I had been playing. I felt badly about that. On one hand, it was prideful for me personally. But on the other hand, I also knew I had let the team down by not working hard in the classroom.

This period of ineligibility forced me to do better. I was waking up on time, going to class and doing my homework. It was during this time that I developed a meaningful relationship with our team chaplain, Rev. Ronald Smith. He helped me a lot and became a great influence on me. I started going to church with him. When he would preach at different churches in the surrounding communities, he would take me with him and introduce me to lots of people. He gave me money, fed me and bought me clothes. Rev. Smith helped me get my driver's license. He even bought a car for me to drive. He gave me a lot of structure, too. I would live with the chaplain during the week and then go home on the weekends to Willowood. Later on, he signed paperwork and legally adopted me. He would often speak of me as "his son." It felt good to hear someone call me his son. However, in the back of my mind, I knew I had only one daddy. Absolutely no one could take his place in my life.

My hard work in the fall semester paid off. My grades improved so well that when January rolled around, I was ready to play. The last half of the season I dominated the court! My first game back was against Monroe, the school where I had been suspended the previous summer. I had not forgotten what happened there during the summer term. I was out to avenge the treatment I had received from their principal. The headlines of our local newspaper (Albany Herald) read, "He's Back!" We took up where we left off.

The fan base for Albany basketball overall had begun to grow because our four high schools had the best basketball teams in the state of Georgia at that time. All of us were going deep into the state tournaments, and the people in Albany were excited to be part of it. The high school games were so popular that the local high school gyms were too small to handle the crowds. Our local civic center seats 10,000 people, and it would sell out for the high school games. The people in the stands would go wild at every game. It was exciting.

Our Westover fans were the best. They showed up at every game and gave our team 100 percent support. However, the opposing schools hated me as much as the Westover fans loved me. Other teams would pick a fight to get me kicked out of games. Their fans called me names and said a lot of nasty things. They started rumors about me. Facing strong opposition comes with being a superstar. I was learning to live with it. However, it would sometimes go too far. Although I was 6'8" and 240 pounds, I was still only 16 years old. People forgot that. Coach B always told me I was a "man child," meaning I had the body of a man but the innocence of a teenager.

During my sophomore year, we went 25-5. We defended our state championship title against Southside High School from Atlanta and their superstar forward, James Forrest. He had been named Mr. Georgia Basketball for two consecutive years and eventually played for Georgia Tech. The game was in the Albany Civic Center. Southside had beaten Dougherty High School (an Albany rival) the night before. James scored 50 points against Dougherty. However, we got the best of them and won. I was named MVP of the game. Once again, Westover was the best team in 3A basketball in Georgia.

Chapter 8

My junior year was special. I paid attention in class, did my homework and my grades remained steady. I was able to play the entire season. I was considered among the top five players in the world and the number one power forward in the nation. I was named Mr. Georgia Basketball that year. I was the first player from Albany ever selected. I was named a Parade All -American, the highest award for a high school basketball player and was invited to the Adidas All-American camp that summer. Many colleges in the nation wanted me. And my ego was through the roof. I was writing history. I realized I had achieved everything my brother had. I was getting the shine he had gotten when I was in middle school. I had the notoriety, the clothes and the girls. I loved it.

Our season ended at the same place it had ended two years in a row, the state championship. We played in the finals against St. Pius X High School from Atlanta and blew them out in the Albany Civic Center. For the third consecutive year Westover was the reigning champion and it felt great. We had put Albany on the map in the basketball world.

I still had my challenges off the court. One of my major difficulties was trust issues. For instance, I began to feel some distance from the chaplain during my junior year. Part of it was that he was engaged, and I got the impression his fiancé did not want me around. Oddly, I felt like he was trying to pull me away from my mom and brother. I was not about to let that happen. It all felt wrong to me. They were my family, and he would not come between me and them. My godmothers felt uncertain about Rev. Smith, too. As I look back, the favoritism he showed toward me felt wrong. Most of the players on our team were from very similar situations as my own, but he did not help them. That partiality created some jealousy on our team. I felt like he was helping me for his sake, not for mine. My trust in others took another hit.

Our relationship was strained further because of an incident that happened in the fall of my junior year. I was staying with the chaplain during the week. He had gone to a football game one Friday evening, and we had discussed that I would come later. When I didn't show up for the game, he came back home. When he did, he discovered I was still there and I had invited a lady to come over. When she heard him come in, she hid in the closet and he found her. He was so angry about the situation that he told me to get my things and to move out right then. I was no longer welcome there. He also took away the car he had given me to drive. Our relationship was rocky from that point forward.

The specific situation continued and took a bad turn because when the girl left the chaplain's house, she stole my jersey. I couldn't find it, and I couldn't find her. Our team photo shoot was coming up. My godsisters and godmothers were determined to find that jersey. They weren't playing. We located my jersey, but only after the photos were taken. Once again I was taken advantage of by someone I thought I could trust.

My true friends stayed close. I don't think it mattered to them if I was a celebrity athlete. Eric was that kind of friend. Eric was not a hustler, nor was he trying to help me for his own sake. Even though he was Cooch's older brother, he was a good guy. His mom, Ms. Fannie, has been a special help to me as well through the years. During my darkest days, both of them were there for me.

One of my best friends was (and still is) a guy we called "Manute." His real name is Antonio Smith. We called him Manute because he reminded us of Manute Bol, who at the time was the tallest player to ever play in the NBA. Antonio was shaped like Manute. He and I were the only players to be on all four of the Westover state championship teams. In fact, Antonio was on my team at Southside when we won the Albany middle school championship in the eighth grade. Antonio was a great guy who handled himself gracefully. He never had the issues I did. He had both of his parents, who were supportive. However, he would steal Kool cigarettes from his dad for me. I would send my little brother to his house to get them. Antonio would go on to play at Louisiana Tech University.

Life was getting better and better with each state championship. In my eyes, I had it all. I had money in my pockets, nice clothes, good friends to hang with and a car to drive. I could go and do as I pleased. I began to see myself as the man of the house. I was a grown man physically and in many ways, I felt like I was equal to my mom as an adult. No one could tell me what to do. Everything seemed easy, and I felt invincible. I was all of 17 years old.

However, I learned that things can change quickly. One unforgettable incident stands out. One night I was hanging with my crew going to different clubs. Even though I was a minor I was still able to get into nightclubs. That's one of the benefits of being a celebrity. People want you around because you bring the crowds with you. Our crew was out drinking and smoking mass amounts of weed on this particular night. Another crew was at the same club when a misunderstanding occurred between us in the parking log. In the heat of the moment, someone pulled out a gun and shots were fired. My big homie, Pokey, was hit in the leg by one of those shots. Another friend and teammate, Willie Sessions, was shot in the finger. I remember hearing the bullets whiz by in the air. I turned and ran several blocks into a neighborhood behind the club. I stopped and knocked on several people's doors so I could hide because I was frightened. Man, that incident was scary! Pokey had been a close homie and I hated Pokey getting shot. We hung tight!

When I finished my junior year with another state title, the big question was being asked everywhere I went: Where would I go to college? I was having college recruiters from all over calling me. Although I had verbally committed to the University of Cincinnati, other schools kept trying to get me to change my mind. I had many of those schools' boosters send me money and gifts through the mail and Western Union. I was basically supporting my family financially. I wanted to go to the pros straight out of high school because I knew I would make a lot of money, but that was against the rules of the NBA. Coach B also thought it was best for me to have a year of college ball. I was excited to attend the University of Cincinnati, where I would play for Coach Bob Huggins. I had attended a camp there and fell in love with the school. They had played in the Final Four against the famed Michigan Fab Five. I liked what I saw. I was ready to go. I needed to go.

Chapter 9

As I entered my senior year, I felt like I was an all-world basketball star on the court. We were the three-time state champions. No Georgia high school team had ever won four titles in a row, and we were determined we would be the first. Though we were the number one team in the state, on a national level it was a different story. We were invited to play in a national tournament because of our success the previous three years, but our guys were just not ready. They had not been field tested against such talent. I remember playing in Myrtle Beach in a tournament against other nationally ranked teams like Simon Gratz, a high school in Philadelphia. My fellow McDonald's All-American teammate, Rasheed Wallace, played on their team. They beat us and, as a result, my chances of winning the National Player of the Year began to fade.

However, my teammates had improved their game and many of them were being recruited by colleges. My buddy, Manute, had developed his skills since our freshman year. We were always pushing each other. I felt like I had to perform the best at each game. For three years, I had been the "go to" man, but now my teammates had improved their game so Patriot basketball was not centered solely around me anymore. I focused on leading the team in scoring and rebounds. I wanted to dunk on anyone and everyone. If I didn't, I was not happy.

We played great during the second half of the season as we made our run to a fourth state title. Our team was determined we would get it. It was a dream Manute and I had dreamed ever since middle school. As kids, he and I had talked most every day about becoming legendary ball players, especially as we got closer to high school. Both of us felt that we could play on varsity squad even as freshmen, which was unheard of in our day. Freshmen usually played on the B team, not the varsity, but he and I both stepped onto the court as varsity players. Our dreams were coming true. We just didn't know four state championships were possible.

We eventually made our way to the semifinals of the state tournament. Even though it was not the championship game, it would prove to be pivotal to me, the team and our pursuit of a fourth state title.

Our opponent in the final four game was Lithonia High School. I was getting fouled by them, but the referees were not calling the fouls. Coach B was even on the refs trying to get them to call the fouls, but they refused. I came to a point where I had had enough and I cussed the referee. As a result, he called not only one technical on me, but a double technical. That kind of call never happened, especially in the state playoffs. However, because of those two technicals, I was ruled ineligible to play in the next game, which meant if we won, I would not play in the championship game. It would be one of the greatest moments in Georgia high school basketball and my last game as a Westover Patriot, but I would not be a part of it. I would sit with the rest of the team and watch from the bench. I was depressed and I was angry. We did win the semifinal game, and while I was excited about our win, I also felt like I had been cheated out of this moment.

After that game and the technicals, I was stressed out. I did the only thing I knew to do to deal with it. Coach Boston had chosen to house our team in a local hotel that weekend, even though we were in our home town. However, that didn't stop me from heading out and hanging with my friends. We smoked some heavy weed late into the night. We returned to our rooms, and the next day I smoked so much weed I was high as a kite by the tip-off.

Our opponents in the game was our hometown rival, Albany High School. We had beaten them in the championship game my freshman year. However, they had beaten us twice that season.

My friend, Melvin Drake, a.k.a. Poochie, played for the Indians. Yes, it was Drake again. This time he had a flat top. This was another reason I was disappointed about not playing. I did not want Poochie to win a state championship against me. I wanted to win all four. I could do nothing about it except cheer on my teammates.

Albany High had also picked up another great player, Michael Spruell. They were determined to dethrone us, and we were just as determined to "four-peat" as state champions. The team that played the best that night would win. With Westover's best player on the bench, the outcome was up in the air. The rematch was played at the Albany Civic Center, and boy was it packed to the last seat. The arena was electric with excitement. Our guys wanted to win this game badly without me. They wanted to show themselves and the watching world they could win without me. Few people thought we would win, but Coach B led our team well and they responded. They played together as one team and when the final horn sounded, we had won and was crowned state champions for the fourth straight year. We had just made history and became known as the "Quad Squad" for having won four straight titles. I was relieved. The celebration for our team, our school and our fans was off the chain.

Something meaningful happened that night after the game that I still remember fondly. Throughout the season, I had honestly felt some distance from the other teammates. I don't know what it was, but when they won that state championship without me, I felt close to them again.

Chapter 10

At the same time my life on the court was making history, my life off the court was a different story. I was feeling a lot of pressure. I was depressed and anxious and I didn't know how to deal with it. I thought it was just a part of my journey. I was worried about a lot of things. First of all, I had two infant daughters and a son on the way. I was anxious about what would happen to them after I left for college. I felt like I had to take care of my family and my whole circle of friends, including the people who had taken care of me all along the way. To me, this meant only one thing. I had to earn as much money as I could as quickly as I could. I needed to get to the pros fast. Looking back, it was unnecessary pressure I had put on myself.

I was being pressured to choose a college to attend because I had not officially signed with Cincinnati, and other schools were still recruiting me. I was constantly thinking about "What if?" What if I didn't perform well? What if I got hurt? What if I couldn't graduate? What if we didn't win the fourth state championship? What if I failed the SAT and had to sit my freshman year? I was hoping to be the first person from Albany to play in the NBA, but what if I didn't make it? How would Albany look at me then? I was representing the city, and I did not want to fail my hometown.

My final year of school was a continuation of the previous three years. I had too many unexcused absences to graduate. The principal and I did not get along, which was disappointing to me. I felt like I had brought a lot of notoriety to Westover, but he did not seem to appreciate it. School attendance felt useless because I knew I would not graduate from there. I walked around with a chip on my shoulder, feeling like I could do whatever I wanted. I cussed out teachers. I skipped classes except on game days. On other days, I remember just getting up and leaving school. Somehow, Coach B kept me from being suspended. I would go hang out around town. I hated school, but I look back now and wish I had enjoyed it.

I did not like being around crowds, but I did not like being alone either. Both situations made me nervous. What made it even harder was I had very few people I could talk to. I did not want anyone to think I was weak. I also enjoyed spending time with Mrs. G over lunch. She would listen to me talk about all of my hang-ups. Deon Payton was a leader on our girls team. She was one of the few people I felt like I could trust. She also was responsible for probably saving my life and my future by keeping me from making a reckless decision one day at school.

It happened during P.E. Several of us were playing a pickup game in the gym when things got out of hand. Words were exchanged and in just a moment, fists began to fly. Willie Sessions, one of my teammates, threw an uppercut from out of nowhere to my chin and I started bleeding. The other guys stepped up and broke up our fight. I was so angry that I stormed off the court and went out to my car and got my gun that I always kept in my car. I intended to take care of business. When I began walking back toward the gym, Deon was there and she stopped me. "Don, what are you doing?!" I stopped and we talked. I decided to take my gun back to my car.

While I brought a lot of this pressure on myself, I also felt a lot of pressure from the celebrity status I was carrying. I was a top five player in the nation. I was a McDonald's All-American and the best player in Georgia. I was featured in different magazines. I had led our team to a fourth state title. Since I was in the national spotlight, I was no longer competing against other local stars. I felt the pressure of competing against the likes of Jerry Stackhouse and Rasheed Wallace. All the shine I had wanted while living in the shadow of my brother had now come to me. As a 17-year-old kid, I didn't realize how hard it was.

I had three answers to dealing with all of the pressure - basketball, weed and sex. Those habits kept my mind occupied, and I was able to mask the anxiety eating me from the inside.

My thirst for sex became addictive. I always had a girl at my side. Vel and I would get hotel rooms and just hang out with different college girls. It was around this time I began a sexual relationship with a well-respected high school teacher. I seldom had a good night's sleep. I was even having sex at school, sometimes twice a day. I'll be honest and admit my craving for sex began when I was in middle school. I remember many nights when my mom was working that my older brother, Banastrues, would have a girlfriend over. I would sneak into the living room where they were having sex and watch, unknown to them. It was the beginning of another powerful addiction.

I was drinking a lot of liquor also. Hennessy was the drink of choice for us. I was smoking weed all the time. I would get together with my friends for "smoking sessions," where we would roll up marijuana in a cigar wrapper instead of papers. You can get more weed in a cigar so it would last longer. We called them "blunts." When I went to school, I was always high. I would smoke a joint before classes. I felt like I couldn't function without it. So there was basketball, weed and sex. Those were my priorities. Grades and learning were very low on the list. Everyone knew my night life was off the chain. They knew I needed structure. That's what Coach B and the team chaplain kept trying to tell me, but I would not listen.

It became increasingly obvious to me and to others that I would not fulfill the graduation requirements that spring. My extended family arranged for me to finish high school in Cincinnati, Ohio. After we won the state championship game, I knew I was not graduating from Westover, so I stopped attending school altogether. I just hung out with my crew and lived it up for about a month. Later in the spring, I played against other great players in the nation in the McDonald's All-American game. I scored a double-double with 13 points and 13 rebounds.

It was during this time a situation occurred that would haunt me for the rest of my basketball career. One morning, I needed to go somewhere and my godsister was using her car. When my mom got home from work, I asked to borrow her car.

For some reason, she said no. I hadn't heard no from any adult or anybody for years! I didn't handle the situation correctly. My mom and I had a huge argument, and I became so upset I knocked over a kitchen cabinet. This cabinet had been in our family since I can remember. It fell to the floor along with everything in it. The plates smashed into pieces. Although she was small, my mom would not let anyone walk over her, including her 6-foot-8 superstar son. She called the police! I couldn't believe that. (Looking back, I don't blame her.) When the police officer arrived, I totally disrespected him. When he tried to put me in handcuffs, I refused! It was an all-out wrestling match. The officer won, and I spent my first night in jail. Although the incident made the local headlines and the news in Cincinnati, the word-of-mouth news traveled faster around Albany. Most of that news was simply wrong. People were saying I had hit my mom. I was being painted as a criminal. I never did hit my mom. I will admit I responded to my mom and the police officer wrongly, but I was no criminal. It was crazy!

The rumors were ruthless. For a 17-year-old, I did not understand why people were saying these things.

I was in jail for two days awaiting a hearing. A lawyer named Bob Beauchamp voluntarily came to the jail to represent me. He was very helpful during this time. I remember him bringing me breakfast sandwiches on the morning of my court appearance. He and his family even invited me to their home for dinner afterwards. He was a nice guy. However, I'll confess that his wife's cooking had no taste to me. I thought she had cooked some greens for the meal, but I didn't see any fatback in them. My mom always cooked fatback in her greens. When I tasted them, I thought to myself, "What the hell is that?" Spinach. It was spinach!

My mom came to my side and stood up for me as well. She wanted people to know the truth about the whole situation. Our family had taken a hit with this incident, and it was our goal to just get the situation behind us. I was charged with resisting arrest and assaulting an officer. Mr. Beauchamp told me if I pleaded guilty, there would be no further time to serve in jail. I was good with that. All I wanted to do was get out of jail, get out of Albany and head to Cincy. But when I stood in front of the judge, he decided to give me additional time behind bars! He said I could serve the time once I returned from Cincinnati for the holidays. That decision was unbelievable to me. However, it was over and that was what mattered. I was off to Cincinnati and to a new start. I was ready for it.

Best Players in Albany - 1993

Going against Rasheed
Wallace in Myrtle Beach

Coach Willie Boston

One and Done

Chapter 11

About a week after the hearing, Rev. Smith pulled up to our apartment on Friendship Street early on a spring morning. He was taking me to Cincinnati. While I had hoped my godsister would take me, my support system thought it was best if I rode with the chaplain so I didn't say anything. He had also told me he would take me shopping, and I did not want to miss out on that.

It was the last time I would see my Willowood neighborhood for a very long time. I had been away from home before, but not for this length of time. I was sad to be leaving because I would miss my family, but it was the best route for me to go. Along with my mom, brother and grandmother, my friends and extended family were there to see me off. I had private moments prior to this morning when I cried about leaving them, but I could not show my real emotions in front of others because that felt like weakness to me, which was the opposite of what my dad had taught me about being tough.

Not only were my suitcases packed, but so were my socks. I had stuffed weed in one sock and I had stuffed a few hundred dollars in the other sock. Before I left Albany, I gave my mom $300. It felt good giving that money to her, especially with the bad rumors swirling around our family. All of my life I have wanted to make my mom proud. I personally have never heard her brag on me, but people always told me she did. My mom is the strongest person I know. She is physically small, but don't be fooled by her size because her strength is undeniable. So is her love. My mom has worked extremely hard for us over the years. I remember during my high school years she worked at a Hardee's at night. During the basketball season, she and I would often ride to my home games together and then I would take her to work afterward. She never missed a game either. Then I would have to get up early the next morning and pick her up. One of the best parts was the cinnamon raisin biscuits she would have waiting for me. I also remember seeing my mother not eat with us when we were younger. It was not until I was older that I realized why. She wanted to make sure we ate so she would often go without for us. She was, and still is, a great mom.

Rev. Smith and I headed north to Cincinnati that spring morning. We stopped in Atlanta and shopped for clothes, shoes and everything I needed. It had been almost a year since he and I had a one-on-one conversation. I felt like he took me shopping to ease the tension between us. But I did not get it. He was trying to reconcile with me, and all my 17-year-old brain could think about was the car he took back. "Why did you take away my car from me and give it to another teammate?" I did not understand.

It was arranged for me to move in with the Byrd family. They had a young son and lived in Forest Park, a suburb of Cincinnati. Their large basement would be my home. Since Mr. Byrd worked construction in downtown Cincinnati, he would drive me to school every day on his way to work. The change of scenery was hard for me as a teenager. Cincinnati was a much larger city than Albany, which made me realize how small Albany truly was. I'm not certain I had ever been in a basement before moving in with the Byrds. We didn't have them in south Georgia. They talked funny. Their chili involved spaghetti noodles. They had small yards. All of those differences together were a big change for this teenage boy. It took me a while to adjust. But those changes were only on the surface. Other changes were more challenging.

Honestly, living with the Byrds was a struggle for me. They were good people, but they were different from my south Georgia upbringing. After all, they had house rules. I had not lived under any rules in a very long time. I got tired of them quickly and had a few run-ins with Mr. Byrd, but nothing major. I also got tired of living in a basement by myself. I felt isolated. The move to Cincinnati also involved structure and routines because I had to study for the SAT test every single day. I had not done any type of classwork in a very long time.

I was not as interested in preparing for the SAT or graduation as I was trying to find weed. It was not long before my sock stuffed with weed was empty. I felt like I needed the weed to deal with the stress of the changes going on. Being new to the area meant I had to find a supplier.

Chapter 12

I was enrolled in Robert Taft High School. It was right in the hood with the projects on one side and the police station on the other side. Taft was cool though. It seemed like everyone had heard I was coming. They stared at me because I was from the south. I was country to them. Not only was I the new guy in school, but I was also the famous new guy in school with tight clothes. The University of Cincinnati Bearcats were the talk of the city because they had recently played in the Final Four against Michigan's Fab Five. Consequently, the Cincinnati news talked about me a lot. Now UC was getting the highest recruit ever and the best power forward in the nation, so everyone at Taft High knew about me. I was a future star and their first one and done.

Unfortunately not all of the news about me was good. The rumors about my situation back home in Albany with the police had followed me to Cincy. I was somewhat embarrassed by it all, so I stayed to myself at Taft.

I called home a lot and was able to talk with my mom to see how she and my little brother were doing. I checked in with my baby mamas, too. They were constantly asking me when I was coming home and if I was going to spend time with them. I was a terrible liar and womanizer. It was impossible to deal with these three women when I went back to Albany, so I told them what they wanted to hear.

I felt no reason to stop seeing other girls once I moved. The Cincinnati girls found me interesting, and I didn't mind that one bit. Cincinnati was a new experience in another way for me. Back home, it was highly unusual for blacks and whites to date. We just did not do that. However, in Cincinnati, it was not unusual. I met a couple of white girls and started hanging out with them. I enjoyed spending time with them, but it was very odd for me. I could not adjust to having white girls as friends so I kept our relationships private. Instead of meeting them in restaurants, I would go to their houses or have them come to mine.

I hardly played any basketball during the few months I was at Taft High. I had two goals while I was there. One was to prepare for and to pass the SAT test. That was a requirement for me to further my basketball career. If I was to play basketball at the next level, I had to enroll in college and to enroll in college I had to pass the SAT exam. I attended awesome workshops that taught me different testing strategies. When the morning of the test arrived, it took me back to the last time I had taken the SAT. That first test was given at Albany High School on a Saturday morning after we had played a game the night before. I was so tired that I fell asleep during the test! It was a terrible experience, but this time was different because someone had helped me prepare. I was ready. I took the test and I passed! Honestly, I was surprised, but happy. I would be able to enroll in the University of Cincinnati. It would be a one-and-done year for me!

My mom, my younger brother, Shelton, and my godsister, Debra, came to Cincinnati to attend my high school graduation, which was my second goal. Having my mom at my graduation was a good feeling because I wanted her to be proud of me. And she was, despite the stories that others were spreading. She and I knew the truth. Graduation also meant I was one step closer to providing for my family, especially my mom. She had worked hard all of my life to provide for us, and I couldn't wait for her to not have to work and to have a new home! That was my top priority.

One couple who meant a lot to me during this transitional time was Bobby and Sharon Kortsen. They were high school basketball enthusiasts in Ohio. Westover was a hot bed of talent in the 1990s, so he knew about our school. Mr. Kortsen had invited me to a summer camp in Cincinnati the summer of my sophomore year in high school. It was the first time I had been there and I loved it. He took several of us Albany players to Costa Rica for a tournament the summer before my junior year, including Drake, Manute and Spruell. We played against professional players and though they beat the brakes off of us, it was a great experience.

The Kortsens did something amazing for me by putting together an all-star game in my hometown of Albany that spring. Unfortunately, it was scheduled at the same time as the Magic Johnson Classic where I had been invited to play. I had to decide which one I would play, and I chose to play in my hometown.

Chapter 13

After finishing at Taft with my high school diploma, I moved in with one of the team trainers because he lived closer to campus. However, that move did not go well. My sock of weed was empty, and I needed to find some. He knew people who could help me get it. I also had to pressure him to let me smoke in the apartment. I kept his apartment filled with smoke. Like I said earlier, it didn't go well.

Once the summer started, I moved in with two former players still living in Cincinnati, T. Gib and Lue. I had great respect for them. They were the first UC guys I met, and they showed me the do's and don'ts of Cincinnati. As the summer progressed, other recruits started arriving including Damon Flint, Darnell Burton, Marko Wright, Jackson Julson and Brian Wolfe. Damon was a Cincinnati native and a fellow McDonald's All-

American. We had played together in camps during high school since he was a top 25 player. He and I traveled to Tampa, FL during the summer to play in an AAU tournament. We also had a summer league of college and professional players in the Cincinnati area. Our games at Purcell High School were packed with fans. The Cincinnati media were giving our team a lot of hype after the previous two years of success. Once again, I was the center of attention and once again, the popularity had two sides. On the positive, everywhere I went, people would ask for autographs. On the negative, people knew my every move. For instance, when I returned to Albany before the season started, I had to go to court. It was the talk of Cincinnati. It was like everyone knew about it! I had to decide not to listen to the rumors but instead, to hold my head up and move forward.

I had my first summer job that year, too. Business owners around Cincinnati liked to hire the ballplayers. Many of them were alumni. The university had arranged for us to get jobs. I went to work at a local restaurant cleaning off tables. I ate good, but I remember thinking to myself, "I don't need no job!"

It was a great first summer for me in Cincinnati. I began building friendships with the other players on the team, so when the fall semester started we had become close friends. My first night on campus was memorable. We went out to a club called Primetime, which was properly named. We had a great time, and we all came home with a girl on our arm that night. Primetime was also where I met Nick Van Exel. He had led the Bearcats to the Final Four and the Elite Eight the previous two years. He had just been drafted by the Lakers that summer. He was my first hundred-dollar handshake. When I shook hands with him and pulled back my hand, it had a hundred dollar bill in it. In fact, he did that for every freshman in the club that night.

I also met Corie Blount early on at UC, too. Along with Nick, he was a Bearcat alumnus who had been chosen by the Chicago Bulls in the first round of the 1993 NBA draft.

Chapter 14

Once the training began, I quickly realized basketball at this level was very different than high school. The guys I was competing against at Cincinnati were better, stronger and faster. All of my life I had relied on my size and natural talent because I had always been bigger and better than everyone else. But not here. I couldn't do that anymore. Also, the opposing teams studied you harder. They watched film to discover your tendencies and to exploit your weaknesses on the court. I had to stay locked in if I were to succeed.

The training with Huggins and his staff was like nothing I had ever witnessed. The pre-season conditioning was incredibly hard. I had never lifted weights at Westover. Although Coach B required all of the players to run cross country, I skipped that stuff. But now I was being required to run and to lift weights and could no longer skip out. UC coaches required us to run a few miles before practice under a specific time. I was not able to even finish the first run. I knew if I was to succeed at Cincy, I had to work on my game. And I did. I welcomed the challenges and stepped up my game. College basketball was a big adjustment, but I loved playing the game so I focused on doing what I had to do to get better and stronger in order to compete and to excel.

Only the best made it to this level of basketball, and only the best of the best competed. College basketball was no joke. It was business. One incident proved that to me. My fellow freshman teammate from Georgia was a guy named Marko Wright. He was suspended from the team for a violation I honestly don't recall. I do remember the whole situation did not sit well with me, and basketball was more than a hobby. It was serious!

However, we were still teenagers for the most part. When practices were over and we were left on our own, most of the team couldn't wait to get a beer. But not me. Instead, I went for the weed. Since I was the only player who smoked, I would always break off to my own room. If we were going to sit around, then I was going to smoke weed. To everyone else, the weed was taboo, but I was a functioning weed head! That was my way to cope with the stress. It allowed me to relax.

Although I was far away from Albany, the pressures of Albany were not far from me. I still felt the weight of being a father to my children and taking care of my mom and brother. They were on my mind all of the time. After all, I was in Cincinnati living the good life, eating well, hanging out with friends, sleeping in a nice dorm with money in my pocket and playing basketball while my mom, my brother, my children and their moms were still struggling. That played on my mind a lot during those days in Cincinnati. The weed helped me cope with it all.

Chapter 15

After a hard preseason of workouts and practices, the first game arrived. Everyone had great expectations of our season. I was excited. The great Oscar Robertson was there for the opener. It was a humbling moment when I met him, a UC alumnus and legendary NBA hall of famer. My first game against Butler University was excellent, scoring 32 points and grabbing 12 rebounds. A double-double! I broke the Big O's freshman record! I had made history already in my first game. I was on my way. We won 90-72.

The next game we played was in the Dean Dome in Chapel Hill, North Carolina. Growing up, I remember watching Dean Smith and the Tar Heels on television, and now I was playing them. My fellow McDonald's All-American, Rasheed Wallace, was on their team along with Jerry Stackhouse and Jeff

McInnis. Rasheed was a monster. We lost, 90-63. I was no stranger to playing in front of large and loud crowds, but that game in the Dean Dome made me realize how much better it is to play in your own arena rather than on the road. It was intimidating playing in front of those Carolina fans. I remember the technical foul I received during that game. Play had stopped, and I was frustrated by it all. Instead of handing the ball to the referee, I mindlessly tossed the basketball up in the air. All of those fans went wild immediately, and the referee blew his whistle and hit me with a tech.

One of the biggest games that year was against Xavier University, our crosstown rival. It was rivalry week on ESPN, and it was televised nationwide so the game was not only the talk of Cincy, but it had the attention of people around the nation. I had injured my foot earlier in the season with a stress fracture. I had returned two games earlier and had excelled with 19 rebounds in each game. However, I had also aggravated the fracture. I was in pain, but I was not going to complain because I wanted to play! But I also knew I couldn't explode while playing like I normally had. We were down at halftime, and Coach Huggins fussed and cussed at us, specifically calling me out. Yelling has never done anything for me, and I responded in a disrespectful manner to him. I felt like I was doing my best, and he was not respecting the fact that my foot was not healed totally. We ended up losing, 82-76, and after that loss, I was telling myself that I was going pro after this season for sure.

The season was up and down, but we pulled it altogether and ended up going 22-10. We won our conference championship. I averaged 16 points and nine rebounds a game during the season. I was chosen as the Great Midwest Conference Newcomer of the Year and was named to the all-conference second team. I was among the conference leaders in points and rebounds.

Just as Coach B had made a lasting impression on me at Westover, Coach Bob Huggins, a.k.a. Huggs, made an impression on me at Cincy. He had built a successful basketball program there, having gone deep into the NCAA tournament the two years prior to me coming. The Bearcats won 12 of 13 conference titles during his tenure. He was the kind of coach who would holler and fuss at me, but then later he would come up and put his arm around me and tell me he loved me. As a 19-year-old, I had never had that kind of coach before. That was strange! He was very supportive of me, and at the end of that first year made the case to the media about placing me on the first all-conference team. Huggs took up for me, and I gained much respect for him because of that. He was hard on us, but he knew we needed it if we were to excel. Today, I look back and realize how good of a coach he was to us. He truly cared about us as players and as people.

One incident stands out. We ate our team meals in the Shoemaker Center, a restaurant in the arena. It was usually baked chicken. I complained about it to Huggs, and he said to tell him what I wanted. I did and the menu was changed! I thought that was great.

Our conference championship secured our place in the NCAA Tournament. I wanted to play well because we would be in the national spotlight, and this kind of exposure can make you or break you. We played the first round in Ogden, UT against Wisconsin and, unfortunately, we lost, 80-72. Although I had a double-double (20 points and 10 rebounds), our team overall did not play well. My first and only season of college basketball had come and gone. It was over.

Chapter 16

When I returned to Cincinnati, my phone rang from sunup
to sundown. Agents were calling ready for me to decide on the
NBA. They would fly into Cincy every day, and I would meet
them for dinner. Boy, did they wine and dine me! For a 19-year-
old, this was big time.

Coach Huggins was at the tournament finals, and he had
told me we would talk about my future when he returned. He had
no clue I was meeting with agents during this time. I talked to my
roommate, Big Mike, about everything. I wanted to wait and talk
to Huggs about this important decision, but I was impatient. I
kept thinking about my mother and brother struggling back home.
I kept thinking about my four children and another one on the
way. How was I going to provide for them? I was not wanting the
money to live a bigger life. I wanted the money so I could take

care of my family. I was trying to be responsible. And I was not even 20 years old yet! After several days of wrestling over the future, I decided to sign with an agent, and he gave me $10,000 that very day! I also offered to hire Big Mike as my personal trainer. He went with the money, too, and left his senior year of college to go with me on this journey.

I still remember meeting with Huggs after he returned. Honestly, I felt guilty about signing without talking to him. When he returned, he scheduled a meeting with me in his office, and when I told him I had already signed with an agent I think he was speechless. I could tell by the look on his face he was disappointed with my decision. Looking back, I know I would not have decided for the NBA that year if I had talked to him because I valued his advice. At that time, I just wasn't thinking clearly. After a moment, he simply wished me the best and told me we needed to set up a press conference to announce my decision to declare for the draft. We did and after the conference, everyone just walked away, the Cincinnati media, Coach

Huggins, the staff. It felt like a desert. I knew I needed to get out of the UC dorms.

The NBA draft was three months away, and I had to prepare. Since my agent was from New York, Mike and I moved there to train. I moved my pregnant girlfriend from Cincinnati there, too (my son, D.J.). I had heard rumors that another of my Cincy girlfriends was pregnant. But I never made it a point to find out. She did not reach out to me, and I did not reach out to her. I would find out later this child was my fifth, Autumn.

The Cincy press came down hard on me once I declared for the draft. All the love they had for me just a few months earlier had disappeared. They said I was just chasing the money. I thought that was the point! I was going to make it in the NBA and start providing for my family like I had planned all along. My plan was coming together.

At the time I was given a line of credit from my agent. He had also arranged for me to autograph basketball cards with my picture on them. The card company paid for me to sign those cards - - 60,000 of them! That gave me the ability to start taking care of my mom, which was a good thing because of what would happen to my family that summer in Albany.

I trained hard in New York getting ready for the draft combine held in Chicago that year. When I arrived, I roomed with Darrin Hancock, a Georgia legend in basketball. He was the star player on the Griffin High School team that beat my brother in the state playoffs. Darrin had played for the University of Kansas, who had gone to the Final Four that very season. He declared early for the draft, too.

The draft combine was the most competitive event I had ever attended. Everyone was there to secure their place in the NBA. Once again, the level of basketball had stepped up. It was even more serious than college ball. No longer were we competing for a spot on a team. Now everyone was competing for their future in professional basketball. Careers were on the line. I was the youngest player there, just a few weeks shy of my 20th birthday. While I was excited to be at the combine, after a couple of workouts, I began to second-guess my decision to enter the draft. Many of the scouts told me if I had stayed at Cincinnati another year, I could have been player of the year and a guaranteed lottery pick. Hell, I was just happy to be drafted in the first round.

During the combine, I met with Isiah Thomas, a former NBA superstar and future Hall of Famer. At the time, he was working with the up-and-coming expansion team, the Toronto Raptors. I enjoyed our conversation until he asked me a question that caught me totally off guard. Isiah smiled at me with his signature smile and said, "Dontonio, I've heard you burned down your mother's house. Is that true?" I was shocked because I had no idea where that question had come from. I wondered for a second if he was kidding me. Why did he think I had done that? Who had told him that? And did he believe I would do that? What kind of person did he think I was? Burn down my mom's house!? Are you serious? I had never heard that story before. Those terrible lies disguised as rumors had spread all the way from my small town of Albany to the kings of the NBA. The word on the street was that I had burned down my own mother's house. I couldn't believe it. I told him point blank, "Hell no!" I didn't know if he believed me or not. However, the following season when the NBA held an expansion draft for the Toronto Raptors, they chose me. When they did, I felt like Isiah had believed me and not the rumors.

Chapter 17

After the combine, I flew home to Albany for a draft party in Willowood. It was like the whole neighborhood was out celebrating me and my accomplishments. It was this moment when I realized I was the first person to truly make it out of the 'hood and into the spotlight. I would do what no one else in my neighborhood or the entire city had done - play basketball in the NBA, the most talented basketball league in the world. Many kids were looking up to me, and I was only one year out of high school.

My mom had arranged for a big-screen television to be put in the parking lot for everyone to keep up with the draft. The summer had been rainy so we were fortunate the skies cleared that June afternoon. I remember going into my mom's room alone to watch. I did not want anyone in there with me. It was just me and my weed. Although I was anxious and doubtful, at the same time, I was completely confident. I was all over the place. I recall thinking about how I would buy my mom a house and a Lexus. Growing up, she always had car issues, but I was about to change all of that and begin to provide for her. I also thought about my kids, and I was making plans to spoil them. I couldn't wait to see how it would go.

The 1994 draft began with the Milwaukee Bucks picking Glenn Robinson. Guys like Jason Kidd and Grant Hill were picked. During the draft, my agent called and told me the New York Knicks and the Seattle Supersonics were very interested in me. That was cool because both had first round picks. I had had a good workout with the Knicks especially. Seattle had the 11th pick, and they chose Carlos Rogers, a 6'11" center from Tennessee State. New York had two first -round picks. They chose Monty Williams first. Then they had the next to last pick in the first round. My heart was about to beat out of my chest while I was waiting! I was hopeful to hear David Stern, the NBA

Commissioner, call my name. Instead the Knicks chose the All-American point guard from Florida State, Charlie Ward. He had also won the Heisman Trophy that year. Interestingly, he was raised in Thomasville, Georgia, about fifty miles from Albany. We had also worked out together with the Knicks. I was disappointed, to say the least. I remember a tear sliding down the side of my face when I heard his name. That hurt me, but I was determined to hold my head up.

There was a big difference in the first and second rounds of the draft. First round meant a guaranteed spot on the roster and a three-year contract. Second-rounders had no such guarantees. The second round began. The Vice-Commissioner of the NBA walked to the podium on national television to announce the ninth pick of the second round, "The Seattle Supersonics choose Dontonio Wingfield from the University of Cincinnati." When he did, the 'hood exploded! It was like the fourth of July that night in Willowood.

It was not long after the announcement before the Sonics coaching called me welcoming me to the team. After I hung up, it was time to party! I gave my mom a big hug and about that time, my crew showed up. We went to a local night spot called The House of Jazz. I felt the love that night. I felt like Albany knew I was representing them as their first player to be drafted in the NBA and I wanted to make my city proud. Willowood was especially excited. They didn't care I was a second-round pick. They cared about me. They had a guy picked in the NBA draft. No one else in Albany had ever been able to say that. It was a proud moment for Willowood, and we celebrated! It was a night I have not forgotten. When the people you love celebrate you, it is an unforgettable moment.

The Pinnacle

Chapter 18

The summer of '94 was memorable for my hometown. The rains came hard and heavy from Tropical Storm Alberto. A couple of days after the draft I was trying to catch a flight to Atlanta and then to Seattle, but the weather was so bad many of the flights were either cancelled or delayed. The storm dropped more than twenty inches of rain on southwest Georgia and much of Albany was flooded, including Albany's oldest cemetery, causing coffins to pop out of the ground like popcorn. The Washington Homes project, where my grandmother lived, was surrounded by that cemetery. She was flooded and lost all of her possessions. She moved in with my auntie.

When I finally was able to catch a flight to Seattle, it was a flight of many mixed emotions. We taxied down the runway in the pouring rain, and I remember looking down on the flood waters as we rose into the clouds. The Flint River was swallowing my Willowood neighborhood forcing everyone to be evacuated. Many of those families had little or no help in getting their belongings and those families included my mom and brother, my children and their mothers. My mom and brother lost everything, including her car. They had to move in with my Auntie and Uncle in Baconton, a small community about 20 miles away. It was extremely hard leaving them behind in a flood. I still remember a tear rolling down my face. I was especially saddened that the two places where I had grown up were being flooded. Washington Homes never was rebuilt. But I knew I was doing the best thing for them by heading to Seattle. I was flying out to sign a $175,000 contract. That was the best help I could give them. From that point on, I paid most of their expenses because I had the means to do so. That was the main reason I entered the draft. I had people to take care of, and I was going to take care of them. That was important to me.

However, I was also excited because I was about to sign a contract to play in the NBA. I felt like I had finally made it. Our family would never be poor again. The struggle was over. I was barely 20 years old and was about to play with superstars like Sean Kemp and Gary Payton. I had watched these guys on television and now they were my teammates. Yet, I was nervous about the future because I had no idea what the future held. What was on the other side of this door called the NBA? I was at an elite level, a place I had never been. Still, I was confident I would make the team. I knew I would have to work hard and prove myself. The closer I got to Seattle, the more excited I got. It truly was a flight of mixed emotions.

When I arrived, the Supersonics put Mike and me in an upscale hotel in downtown Seattle. It was beautiful, although it rained every day. The highlight of checking in was meeting an NBA legend, Bill Cartwright. While living in Willowood, I remember watching him on TV play with Michael Jordan when the Chicago Bulls won the NBA championship. And now we were teammates! I couldn't believe it!

We began practice the very next day. Bill took me to the practice facility in his platinum Mercedes Benz. I was astonished at the cars in the players' parking lot. I was surprised also with the players who were working out. The practices included more than the drafted players. Players from overseas as well as second-year players vying for a new contract were there. I also learned my spot on the team was not guaranteed until the All Star break in February. That was an eye-opener! However, my agent reassured me that I was safe. He said the General Manager liked me a lot.

I went to Utah to play with other Sonics players in a pro summer league, the Rocky Mountain Review. We actually won the championship! Fortunately, I played well, averaging close to a double double. That summer league experience gave me a great deal of confidence. At that point, I knew I could compete at this level and excel.

I was learning the NBA was more than a basketball game. It was a business. They gave us a hundred dollars per diem while in Utah. I would write letters to my mom and my babies' mamas and include a big chunk of this money. I would send cash money through the mail, and it always arrived safely. My girlfriend was pregnant with D.J. at the time. I was still 20 years old and as much as I wanted to take care of my family, I also dreamed of the kind of car I would get as well as the house I would buy for my mom. But I had little time to dream. The NBA was demanding! Training was serious, and I was thankful that Huggs and the Cincinnati staff had prepared me for the NBA by working me hard the previous year.

Chapter 19

Training camp started early in the fall. All the big dogs arrived and were ready to go. I remember being at the Sonics' training facility when out of nowhere came this "bigger-than-life" voice. Gary Payton was in the house! I honestly felt anxious because it was Gary Payton! I couldn't believe I was his teammate. Shawn Kemp was there, too. He was quieter and worked with me a lot. I spent a lot of time with him because I honored his advice. When we practiced, I held my own, but the funny thing to me was that I was always ending up on the floor. Every single play I would somehow fall. But I was learning from these players I respected. They didn't call me by my name, Don. Instead, they called me "Young Fella" or "Rook."

I finally received my first paycheck for about $15,000. Mike and I moved into a condo in downtown Seattle. However, the next checks were about half of that because I was paying child support for five of my six children. Autumn's mom never asked for one penny. I did not have any contact with her or her mom at that time. However, I was paying support for the others. I was also sending money to my mom and aunt back in Albany. Aunt Janice had three sons, all about the same age as my brother. I was taking care of all of them! All of these people were looking up to me, and that gave me strength. I felt like I had become the man I had been rushing to be. It felt good taking care of my mom. She had not worked since the flood. I was happy to be able to send her money because she had worked hard all of her life. Now it was time for me to provide for her. However, I also used my new wealth to splurge on myself. I bought a Lexus! It was my very first car.

As the basketball season drew near, my pregnant girlfriend flew home to Cincinnati to have D.J. with her family around, which was fine by me because I was focused on the Sonics and my role. It also gave me some free time to wonder around Seattle. And I did! I remember flying my mom and little brother out for a visit. That was a very proud moment for me, to have them visit and enjoy my success in person. It was like a dream come true. We had fun shopping at the mall. While I was there, I noticed an attractive young lady who worked at the department store and I thought to myself, "She won't notice me." I'll admit I used Shelt, my younger brother, as bait by spending big money on him in her area, and before I left the mall, she and I had exchanged numbers. We began hanging out together and I enjoyed my time with her. She was older than me and was very sophisticated. She taught me a lot of lessons. Perhaps my most memorable time with her was our New Year's Eve date at a very expensive restaurant called Ruth Chris' Steakhouse. I had never spent that much money on a meal in one setting.

Unfortunately, I did not possess the relationship tools that would enable me to be completely open with her by telling her about my girlfriend in Cincinnati who had just had D.J. or my daughter, Autumn, and her mom living in Cincinnati, or my three other children living in Albany with their mothers. I never mentioned any of that to her. I basically told her half-truths and lived as if I were single. A couple of months later, she told me the news that she was pregnant with my daughter, London. I couldn't believe it! Every woman I became interested in and cared about would end up pregnant with my child. The great pressure settled in on me as my secret life was growing. I couldn't tell anyone about any of this, including my own mom. I felt like I had to choose and I did not know how. I loved both of these women. I was 20 years old and believed that my success and money from the NBA would fix all of this. Hell, it had so far!

When my paychecks began rolling in, I was paying about $2,500 each month in child support to my six children and their mothers. I had a financial advisor who handled my money, taking care of my bills and keeping up with my finances. I actually only met him in person one time. Whenever I needed money for whatever reason, I would call him.

I flew home during the All Star break. It was great to be back in Albany. I had not been there since the flood. My mom and brother were still living with my auntie. Everywhere I went, people treated me special. I was getting the love from Albany, and it felt good. I was able to buy uniforms for my younger brother's middle school team and that made me proud. However, everyone was wanting to see me, and I just did not have the time. I could only stay for a day. Then I headed to Cincinnati to visit my girlfriend and D.J. At that time, I was not in contact with Autumn's mom and failed to connect with them. I regret that now. Then it was on to Seattle to finish out my rookie season.

I was learning valuable lessons on and off the court. On the court, I was learning the value of patience. When the season began, I rode the bench. My rookie season was the very first time in my entire life I was not getting playing time. I did not want to just be on the team. I wanted to be on the court leading my team to victory. I worked hard with my strength and conditioning coach, Bob Medina. He was always in my ear about getting stronger. I listened to him and worked out. I would talk with Shawn or Vincent Askew about my lack of playing time and how to improve. They would always tell me I was ok. "Trust the process. Wait your turn," they would say. I listened to them because I respected them, but I was very impatient. "Screw the process! I'm ready now!" I was ready to play then, not in the future. To me, playing time equalled success. I wanted to represent Albany well, and I felt like sitting on the bench was not accomplishing that. However, my impatience blinded me to the fact that I was only 20 years old, the youngest player in the NBA. I had a long way to go, and in my own mind I had a short time to get there. What I did not know was just how short my time would be.

My coach, George Karl, was not impressed with me. He did not like rookies anyway, and especially he did not like "one-and-done's." He told me so. He also made it clear that I would not see any playing time. One incident comes to mind. It was a stormy day in the Tacoma area where the Sonics played. They were rebuilding the arena in Seattle, so our games were in Tacoma. On that particular afternoon, a storm rolled in and traffic was terrible. As a rookie, I knew that I not only needed to be on time, I needed to be early so I was always on time! When the tip-off rolled around, I was one of only five players there ready to play. Everyone else had been held up because of the storm. Coach Karl embarrassed me by telling me in front of the other players, staff and coaches in the locker room that he would either forfeit the game or play with four players rather than play me. I took his comments to heart. I hated the way George Karl treated me. He sucked the fun out of basketball. It was the start of my battle with depression.

All of this stress with my career and my "secret" relationships kept mounting up, and I was feeling the pressure. I was not playing as much as I felt like I should. I was also not making as much money as I wanted. Compared to my teammates, I felt broke. I couldn't stand to be alone because it was too depressing. As a result, I did what I had always done in the past when I started feeling depressed. I smoked pot, drank alcohol and had massive amounts of sex. I had the money to spend, and I did. I was regularly flying girls to whatever city I was in, going to clubs (even though I was underage) and smoking blunts. It was the only way I knew to cope.

When the season ended, we had a 57-25 record, earning a fourth seed in the Western Conference playoffs. That was when things got serious. It was like a light switch turned on. The playoffs in Seattle were everything! Our regular season games sold out, so a ticket to the playoffs was a hot item. Seattle loved their Sonics! Our opponent in the opening round was the Los Angeles Lakers and a University of Cincinnati alum, Nick Van Exel. We were supposed to win that series, but the Lakers upset us and our season ended abruptly.

Chapter 20

Not only was the season over, I had no contract for the following year. All of my earnings were gone, too. However, that did not stop me from living it up and doing as I wanted. I kept spending like I still had money coming in. I actually did have a couple of checks to come, and I had a line of credit because of my potential earning power. During the summer, I made trips to Cincinnati, Albany and Disney World! I had never been to the Magic Kingdom. I visited everyone during the couple of weeks I was home, including my children. I did see my dad, who at the time was still struggling with his addictions along with health problems including diabetes.

During the summer, the Sonics sent me to the Pete Newell Big Man Camp in Hawaii, where I was able to develop my skills. I

also played in the NBA summer league and attended the Sonics'
off-season training in Las Vegas.

In 1995, during the off-season, two teams joined the
NBA, the Toronto Raptors and the Vancouver Grizzlies. When
the NBA admits a new team to the league, it holds an expansion
draft, which means the new teams are allowed to choose players
from the existing teams to create a roster. However, existing
teams can protect players from the draft. In 1995, Seattle was
willing to re-sign me, but they would not protect me from the
expansion draft. As a result, Toronto drafted me. So off to
Toronto I went. Isiah Thomas, the general manager for Toronto,
had asked me about burning down my mom's house when we
met at the combine the previous year. For them to draft me meant
he did not believe the rumors about me and that incident back in
Albany. When I met with him, the Raptors offered me a one-year
deal for $275,000. However, it was non-guaranteed, meaning
they could cut me at any time before the All Star break. While I
was happy about the money they offered, I was pissed about the

non-guarantee part of the deal. I took a day to think about it and talk with my agent to see if other offers were on the table. That night, I found out the general manager of the SuperSonics had taken a job in Portland. He offered me the same deal as the Raptors, only it was guaranteed. I passed on Toronto and headed to Portland. I was very happy.

Once I moved to Portland prior to the season to begin training, Mike moved on with his life. My girlfriend at the time, D.J.'s mom, moved with me. We had been together for two years at this point. However, I had many secrets from her and my conscience bothered me a lot. She did know about the kids in Albany, but not about my daughter in Seattle.

We were staying in a motel looking for an apartment when London's mom contacted me. She wanted to bring my baby girl to meet me for the first time. So when they came, I got a room for them across the street from where I was staying with D.J. and her mom. Neither knew about the other. It was all a big secret. Or so I thought. London's mom had filed for child support and when she did, she discovered I was paying child support to five other children and their moms. Obviously, our relationship was over at that point.

I soon had to go to Las Vegas for preseason training for two weeks. As usual, I wanted a woman for company, so I flew Brianna's mom to Vegas from Albany. Afterwards when she returned home, she called me and told me she was pregnant. This was my seventh child, a daughter she would name Jay. I was 21 years of age and already the father of six children (soon to be seven), each of them with a different mom.

I had all of these women in rotation in my crazy world, and they trusted me. Yet I was totally living a lie. When by myself, I would wonder, "How long will I get away with this?" Down inside, I knew all of this would come to an end, but I did not know how or when. This craziness bothered my conscience a lot. But I looked around and it seemed normal to the other players in the NBA. My teammates believed the man was to be dominant, just like my father had raised me. They believed they were the king of their house and could do as they pleased. It was nothing for us to go to a club the night before a game and come out with a woman. In fact, it was a guarantee. It was a pimp mentality that told us we could have as many women as we desired. While that rubbed off on me, still I wondered, didn't that bother their conscience? How did they deal with that? It totally bothered me.

On the court, things were running more smoothly. The Trailblazers had hired a new coach the previous season, P.J. Carlisemo. It was his first head coaching job in the NBA. He had been an assistant coach on the "Dream Team" that had won the gold medal in the 1992 Olympics, and he had had a successful career in the college ranks at Seton Hall University. I was excited that I would see more playing time during my second year and I did. The highlight of that season was our games against Seattle. I enjoyed playing against my former teammates, and we split our games. We made the playoffs that year, but lost in the first round to the Utah Jazz.

Chapter 21

I played well in the series against Utah, and the Trailblazers offered me a two-year, $1.2 million deal. I had doubled my previous contract again. I was excited! I felt like my career was beginning to take off. I quickly started upgrading my life by getting my mom a house of her own and a BMW. I was living large in a new house I leased in Portland. It all felt so good. I invited my family and friends to visit me. Greg Anderson, a.k.a. "Whitebread," a former high school teammate, became my new trainer and made plans to move to Portland for the upcoming season.

It was also during a visit to Albany that summer that I ran into someone from my past. It was the very same girl I mentioned earlier in this book. When I saw this young lady, my mind took me back to Southside Middle School, and I remembered the very first time I laid my eyes on her. She was so beautiful to me, and I could not bring myself to talk to her then because I was a shy middle school boy with nothing to offer her. But my dreams had come to pass because now I was someone special, so I approached her and we talked. Our relationship took off, and I began spoiling her and flying her to Portland or whatever city I was in during the season. She was attending college in Albany and working at a local restaurant. She would leave class and fly to the city where we were playing, and then fly back to Albany the next day. I eventually made her quit work because I enjoyed the time we shared together and I was taking care of her. She was also okay with the fact that I had a girlfriend back in Portland already. I had been crazy about this girl for many years, and now she was loving me in return. It was great! I was able to be honest with her. No need to keep secrets from her. I felt like we had a true emotional connection.

I was excited about the upcoming season. Our team had acquired my former teammate from the McDonald's All-

American year, Rasheed Wallace. I also knew I would get playing time with Coach Carlesimo. The biggest news in the NBA during the offseason was Shaquille O'Neal being traded to the Lakers. Playing against him was a highlight moment for me. I still remember when our teams lined up for the national anthem and I looked over at Shaq, he gave me the nod. Many people were saying I looked like him. I also played against Michael Jordan and the Chicago Bulls that year. He had come back from his attempt to play professional baseball. I remember thinking I just wanted to touch him. Perhaps the most memorable game for me that year was playing against Magic Johnson. He had returned to the Lakers after several years in retirement due to his HIV positive diagnosis. We guarded each other during the game at the Forum in L.A. I was super nervous because I wanted to score on him badly. Whenever we had the ball, he would back off and give me the shot. But I kept missing the shot!

Off the court, D.J.'s mom and I were struggling with our relationship issues. We were both still young, and I was gone a lot due to ballgames and practice during the season. She became pregnant with my eighth child, Donovan. She started feeling homesick during the pregnancy and wanted to move back to Cincinnati. I paid for her to move and to provide for her while awaiting Donovan's arrival the following fall. I did not mind her move at all because my mind was consumed with getting playing time. It also allowed me the opportunity to fly my Albany girlfriend to Portland so I could spend time with her.

The Trail Blazers went 49-33, finishing the season strong with an 11-game winning streak. We headed into the playoffs with momentum. I was excited that I would play in the games and contribute to our success. I was ready! We faced the Lakers in the opening round. It was Kobe's rookie season. I played well against them, but he, Shaq and the rest of the Lakers proved to be too much for us and we lost.

Things were falling into place for me after three challenging years, and I was confident of a long and successful career in the league. I felt good about my contribution to the team. At the same time, I was pressuring myself for more. I wanted more playing time, more money, more success and more fame. And I wanted it right then. You would have thought I was poor because I could not see what I truly had. At the time, I did not realize everything was good. I did not understand it was okay to be in the position I was in. I had never ridden the bench until I reached the NBA, so it was hard for me to sit and watch others play. I had always pictured a high level of success in basketball, but I was not reaching it. I felt like I was failing, even though I was at the elite level of basketball. This perception was only creating more stress and a greater depression in me. I also worried about losing it all by getting in an accident, having an injury or not getting a contract.

At times, I felt like it was the coach's fault. I felt like he was not giving me the playing time I deserved, but he was. P.J. believed in me and gave me the opportunity to get my third contract. I just did not see it. I was too impatient. Years later, I understood that P.J. was actually helping me, but I was blind. I recall one game where we were losing badly and in the closing minutes, P.J. told me to go in. I refused! That's right. I refused to go in the game when the coach asked. Boy, did that put me in the dog house! It took me a month to get back in the rotation. All of the stress and pressure led me to where it always had — more alcohol, more pot and more sex.

Chapter 22

In the fall of 1997, I began my fourth year in the NBA, and it was promising. Major changes to the team were made during the offseason. The management fired P.J. and hired Mike Dunleavy as head coach. Several of the players were traded. Our team was full of forwards. We were all guys who were playing the same position. This is where I learned about the politics of the game. In the NBA, playing time goes to the guys making the most money. Since I was the lowest paid forward on the team, I did not get to play as much. That's the politics of professional sports. Portland was a younger team with great players, good chemistry and a bright future. However, from the time I met Coach Dunleavy, I felt for sure I would not fit in his system. That realization only depressed me further. It was the final year of my contract, and I needed playing time to get another contract, either with Portland or another team. Before long, I wanted nothing to do with Dunleavy because I felt like he did not believe in me. Strangely enough, it was about this time that I began having issues with my back and my depression grew deeper. Around Christmas, the team officially put me on the injured reserve list and I no longer traveled with them. It was becoming clear to everyone that I was not returning to Portland the following year, so my agent began trying to work out a release for me. Even though my money was guaranteed, I was not happy, and I needed something to clear my mind as far as basketball went so Greg and I headed to Las Vegas. We hung out, bought some escorts, gambled, smoked weed and drank alcohol. No one really understood how stressful the seasons were and, of course, I did not tell anyone. I did not want people thinking I was weak and could not handle the pressure.

My agent landed a paying gig for me overseas in Leon, Spain. The team would pay me $100,000 for two months. Still, I didn't want to go, but my agent assured me teams were interested in me for the next year. So off to Spain I went. At first I did well, averaging a double-double playing about 25 minutes per game, which was great, since I could not even understand what the coach would tell us. Two other Americans were on the team. After a month, my back issues started up, and I just could not play through the pain. The team was unhappy because I shut myself down. As a result, I returned to the United States to get another opinion on my back.

I flew to Albany, and my girlfriend and I set up home together. Our relationship had grown. She had quit school to be with me in Spain for a short time. Over time, I had learned to trust her and had told her all of my secrets. She didn't mind my past. My family had accepted her as well. We had a solid relationship because we had connected at an emotional level. I still traveled back and forth to Cincy to see D.J. and Donovan regularly. I was doing my part to take care of my responsibilities with them. Living in Albany also enabled me to spend time with my kids who were living there.

Chapter 23

It was the spring of 1998, and I was working out to stay in shape. I was excited about the upcoming season and wanted plenty of teams interested in a healthy Don. However, the NBA Players' Association and the NBA owners were at odds over a new contract. A lockout was likely, which meant players could not practice, and teams would not pay them until a new agreement could be reached. I had begun cutting back on my lifestyle because of it. I was paying rent and utilities on two apartments (one in Cincinnati and one in Albany). I had five car payments, and I was taking care of my mom and all her bills. I was stressed to the max. All of it came to a breaking point on a trip to Cincy.

I had traveled there to be with my family, D.J., Donovan and their mom. While there, she and I began arguing, and the argument became heated. She had grown tired of my ways of disrespecting her. At one point during the argument, I became so angry that I broke a glass table. I had bought that table and believed I had the right to do whatever I wanted with it. But I learned that was not true. The kids' mom called the police. When they arrived, everything calmed down, until they told me to leave. I refused! So they kept talking to me and giving me opportunities to leave the apartment, but I was too stuck on the fact that I paid the bills and my name was on the lease. I should not be forced to leave. It was my apartment! The officers said differently, and they finally had to mace and cuff me. The ensuing scuffle was wild, and I was beaten badly when I landed in the jail that night. I had to hire a lawyer to get me out on bond. I was charged with felony assault because of the extent of injuries the policemen received. It ended up costing me $5,000, money I could have used to live on.

I rushed back to Albany, and I wondered all day on my drive back what my Albany girlfriend had heard about the incident. When I arrived in Albany, I stopped at a convenience store. When I walked in, I looked at the newspaper section and there it was, my picture was on the front page. Lord, have mercy! My heart dropped. When I walked in our apartment, my girlfriend held up the newspaper and showed me the headline. Plus it was all over the local television news. I couldn't believe it. Now everyone knew about it. And not only that, but they heard it wrong. The story was that I had been charged with domestic violence, which was not true. I had not even touched Kristy, my girlfriend. The charges were related to my scuffle with the policemen. It looked extra bad for me.

At various times throughout my career, I had experienced ill feelings of bad things happening to me. It was driven by the fact that I knew I was not living right, and I was worried that it would cost me eventually. It seemed that my feelings were coming true. In my mind, one bad thing would turn to another bad thing, and it was only going to get worse. I was scared, and my confidence was wavering. My back was still an issue.

Depression was constant. Then my Albany girlfriend had a miscarriage. I didn't even know she was pregnant! I still remember feeling sad seeing the fetus in the toilet that night.

All I did was work out, smoke weed and drink. I was living like a hermit. I kept thinking to myself, "My kids will never know how much I just wanted to be successful. I just wanted a fruitful life for them." I thought money was everything and that if I became rich, then all of the undisciplined things I did would not matter. I was beginning to learn money was not everything.

Several months went by, and negotiations continued between the NBA players and owners. As summer turned to fall, the exhibition games were cancelled. When negotiations broke down further, a portion of the NBA season was cancelled, which was a first. No NBA game had ever been cancelled due to labor dispute. With the entire season at risk of being cancelled, the two sides reached an agreement and the season began a month later.

The 1998-1999 season was only 50 games long. The All Star game was cancelled.

Quickly after the settlement, Miami invited me to a mini-camp. It was tough, and no offer came from it. However, the Bullets did make an offer while I was still in Miami, so I had a new deal, as my agent had assured me. It was a one-year, $800,000 contract. I was in a better place. The future looked promising once again. I decided to head to Albany to share the news with my family.

I had one day to spend there before going to Washington to sign with the Bullets. I wanted to convince my girlfriend I was going to change and do better. I was through with my Cincy girlfriend, and I wanted to let her know. I was 24 years old and the father of eight children by six different women. I needed to do better! However, I had no idea what being a father meant.

It had been a stormy afternoon in Albany. On that last night before heading to D.C., my girlfriend and I were riding around in a red Camaro I had purchased for her. I was planning to drop her off at work later. We had left my grandmother's house and were driving in the rain when out of nowhere, a deer jumped into the road. My girlfriend grabbed the steering wheel to avoid hitting the deer and the car hydroplaned.

1994 Seattle Supersonics

Visiting the Boys' Club
in Portland

Darkness

Chapter 26

"He's dead, ain't he! He's dead, ain't he!" screamed my mom in the emergency room. I had been thrown from the car and seriously injured. I was unable to move or respond. Up to that moment, I had been in a semi-conscious state hearing the doctors and nurses talking. It felt like an out-of-body experience. I heard everything that was said and felt everything that was done to me lying in the ditch under the car, in the ambulance and in the emergency room. I remembered saying repeatedly while lying in the ditch, "Thank you, Jesus," and hearing a guy who stopped to help say, "You better thank Jesus that you're even alive." At some point, I regained consciousness and told my mom I would be okay. However, I could not see what she was seeing. Her son's mangled and broken body was laying on a hospital bed with open wounds and fractured bones being prepped for emergency surgery. Things looked critical for me.

Surgery went as expected. The impact of the wreck had broken my ankles and back. The surgeons had to fuse all of them back together. Fortunately, my girlfriend suffered only minor injuries from the accident. During the initial days of recovery, I began to notice that everyone kept me from seeing a mirror. When I finally looked in a mirror, I realized why. It was like half of my face was gone! Some were uncertain I would even walk again. Even the surgeon was uncertain I would. The pain was excruciating.

My situation only got worse. In the months leading up to the surgery, I had started cutting back on my spending, and so had my mom. She thought it would be okay to take the car insurance off my vehicle since I was moving to Washington and would not be driving that car anymore. I know she did that in an effort to help, but back then I did not understand. As a result, I had no insurance to cover the costs of my medical care. I was furious with her!

Just a few days earlier, I was a 24-year-old heading to the NBA with a new team and a new contract. Things were looking up for me, and I was eager for this new start. And then this happened. In a single moment, my NBA career was over! Everything was over! My idea of being a superhero had all but vanished. I was feeling all kinds of emotions. I was angry. I was depressed. I was afraid. I was discouraged. I would cuss and yell at the hospital staff. I threw my food on the floor. I didn't care. I hated everyone and everything at that point in my life. The only thing that calmed me was strong pain medicine and anti-depressants.

I had other ways of coping which the hospital did not approve. When my friend, Greg, would visit me, he would take me out to my own truck in my wheelchair to smoke some weed. He would drive me around the city for hours. I also had ladies visit me while my girlfriend was at work. The nurses caught me with naked women in my hospital bed trying to have sex. That was when all hell broke loose!

I was fortunate, though, because I had lots of support during my stay. My mom, my grandmother, my girlfriend and others stood by my side during this time. Family and friends were constantly trying to get in to see me. Early on, my mom would have none of that. She put up a "No Visitors" sign. Among the visitors who came was Rev. Smith, the guy who had adopted and mentored me in high school. He didn't hold back either. It was like he couldn't wait to let me know how well he was doing. I teared up after he left, and I was beginning to realize how this life thing worked. And it only embittered me. I only looked forward to getting my pain meds and eventually walking out of the hospital.

I didn't eat much during the recovery and lost more than 100 pounds. I was skin and bones. I was becoming addicted to pain meds. I had bed sores because I couldn't move my legs. Also I was in a back brace to keep me immobile. I stared at the ceiling for weeks. After two months, they stood me on my feet. The pain

was almost more than I could bear.

Chapter 27

After three months, I was so fed up with being in the hospital that I asked for an early release. I couldn't take any more. They granted it. Since I had lost my ability to pay the bills, my girlfriend and I moved into a hotel. At this point, my mom had lost her home and car and had gotten a job. She also moved in with her boyfriend in Willowood. I had applied for indigent care with the hospital to help pay for my medical expenses, but I was so ashamed of needing financial assistance I hated to go to the appointments.

My life continued to spiral downward. All I did was pop pain pills, drink alcohol and smoke weed. I was in a bad place. My mom and my grandma had to bring me food. My mom had to help me to the toilet. I remember sitting in a wheelchair in a house by myself all day long thinking it was all over. I didn't want anyone to see me like this because I could not do anything for myself. I could not even watch basketball on television anymore. I would get mad when I tried to watch games. When I could no longer afford my medicine, I turned to Ecstasy and cocaine. I had to keep that from my girlfriend and my mom, but I think both of them knew. I did not care anymore about myself. I just wanted to die.

Child Support began harassing me as well. I would have to go to court and pay whatever they asked to keep from going to jail. I would see my children at times, but often their moms would not bring them around because they thought I was hiding money, but I wasn't. My relationships with the moms were strained and rightly so because I had lied to them for many years. They had no reason to trust me. When the NBA lockout occurred, all child support was cut off because I had no income, which meant it was a year they did not receive any child support from me. I would send money to my out-of-state kids through Western Union, but that was never counted as child support. Eventually, I got a break. The NBA owed me $60,000, and when I got that check, I was able to pay off some bills and I rented a house where all of us, including me, my girlfriend, my brother and mom, could live.

I also filed for disability, which I thought would be approved easily. After all, my injuries had permanently disabled me from working. It was denied. I did not realize the process would take 10 years before disability would be granted.

There was more. About this time my younger brother had a terrible issue to rise up. Because of some poor choices he had made, he was no longer able to play high school basketball. He was only in the ninth grade and already having grown man problems facing a possible 10-year jail sentence. My court case in Ohio was still pending, and I had to decide whether to pay my lawyer or my brother's lawyer. I chose to put my own situation on the back burner in order to take care of my family. Using money I made from selling weed, I paid his attorney's fees and took a plea deal for myself.

It was less than a year after my accident that I went to Cincinnati for my court date and to begin my six-month sentence at a state penitentiary. I gave my mother enough money to last while I was in prison, and with her job, she would be okay. I went up early to see D.J. and Donovan. On the day before my sentencing, I blacked out while driving and ran into a utility pole. I was not injured, which was fortunate because of my previous accident. However, I missed my court date. When I appeared in court the next day, the news coverage was enormous. It was also embarrassing to me. Just 18 months earlier I was a six-figure NBA player and now I was going to prison walking with a cane. The judge ordered me to spend a night in the county jail because I failed to show up at the appointed time. The next day at my hearing, he sentenced me to serve six months at the Orient Correctional Facility in Orient, Ohio.

While there, I stayed mostly to myself. The other inmates knew of me and they gave me great respect. The prison had a basketball league. A number of inmates were from Cincinnati and they remembered me. We had lots of conversations about my few years in the NBA. They also asked me to coach their team. I did and we won the prison league championship. Little did I know this was only a taste of things to come.

One of the blessings that came from the prison stay was my leg braces. Since I was property of the state of Ohio, they had to buy leg braces for me so I could walk properly. I would never had gotten these braces apart from my prison time because they were expensive and I had no insurance and could not afford them on my own. They enabled me to walk without a cane. I tried to stop my drug habits while I was there. In prison you can get any drug you wish, however, I kept away from everything but weed. I smoked weed, and it led me to a terrible mistake. I was staying in touch with my girlfriend in Albany and my Cincinnati children's mom. I would write them regularly. Once, I wrote them on the same day, but when I put the letters into envelopes, I got them mixed up! Each of them received the letter meant for the other.

By this time, both of them were done with me anyway. The letter mix-up only sealed it.

My departure day from Orient prison finally arrived after six long months in the spring of 2000 when I was released with two years of probation. I traveled to Albany initially. Coach Huggins helped me get a SUV to make the trip home. I applied to get my probation moved to Georgia. I found out my Albany girlfriend had gotten pregnant by a college classmate of hers. That hurt me bad because I felt like she and I had become close. She was one of the truest friends I had. I felt like we had gotten to know each other deeply, and now she had moved on with her life. I was disappointed.

Chapter 28

After a few months I decided to move back to Cincy in an effort to salvage my relationships there. I moved in with my children and their mom, but things were tough. I had no money and could not work to support them. I felt weak. My disability had still not been approved. I was terribly depressed. I was feeling the weight of all I had done to hurt my family with my secrets and lies, and I could not fix any of it. After a few months, we came to the conclusion that life would not work well with me being there. She moved in with her mother while I waited for my probation to be changed so I could move back to Georgia.

I eventually moved to Atlanta to be with Donjuwan's mom. She was a friend from Albany I had known for several years. She had visited me regularly while I was in Cincinnati, and in the process she had gotten pregnant. It was a tough pregnancy, and he was born three months early. She and I were living together in different hotels in Atlanta trying to make it work. I'll be honest and confess I was a straight druggy! I chose to use cocaine and Ecstasy. I met friends who were no good to me. It was a terrible time for all of us. I was depressed and did not care about myself. She was working hard and funding us, including my drug habit. Juwan was in an incubator having a battle of his own trying to live. He weighed 3 pounds. I would go to Emory's Crawford Long Hospital to see him in the NICU. He came home on my birthday in June 2001.

About two years later I decided to leave Juwan and his mom, and I moved back to Albany. I continued my drug habits and hung around people who could help satisfy those habits. I had no place to stay. I would do anything for drugs. I remember the many nights I would sleep on a friend's couch, wake up to go to my grandmother's house for a shower and then back I would go to my friends, where we would start our "parties" about midnight. I was in such a weak state that I did not want my mom to see me, so I stayed away from her as much as possible. Our

relationship grew more distant. However, I knew she was praying

for me. And I needed it! The darkness was great and heavy.

Rescued by Kids

Chapter 29

My mom's prayers were working. I began waking up the morning after our parties with a bad feeling. Although the highs I got from the drugs were amazing, the lows that came after were terribly dark. I was constantly battling my conscience. I was hearing a voice that spoke to me during those bad moments telling me that I was better than this and that I had a life ahead of me. I realized I had a choice during those moments. Either I listen to the voice and get off the drugs or else go back and get high again so I would not hear the voice. For a long time, I just kept getting high. But eventually I had enough and started losing a desire for the drugs. I was ready to quit.

I moved back in with my mom and began to find an inner strength. For the first time in a long time, I truly wanted to live and to do better. I wanted my kids to know me. That single thought helped me to start thinking positively. One of my first steps was to start hanging out with new friends, ones who truly cared about me.

One person who helped motivate me was Bob Beauchamp, the lawyer who had represented me several years earlier through the ordeal with my mom in high school. I reached out to him because I needed help with a disability claim. But even more, I still remember the way he had treated me earlier, and I felt like he could help me again because he cared. Mr. Beauchamp hired me to help in his law firm. But after about three weeks, he called me to his office and gave me bad news. He had to let me go. One of his investigators was the police office who had arrested me during the argument with my mom from high school. He had not forgotten me and felt uncomfortable with me around the office. After all, I had kicked him in the groin during our scuffle. How could he forget me? Mr. Beauchamp asked me what I wanted to do and from that conversation, steered me back to my roots, Henderson Gym. The supervisor at Henderson was

Curtis Marshall. He had worked in the city's recreation department for many years. He welcomed me back to the gym and allowed me to start working with the children. This step was big for him because the rumors around Albany about me were terrible. People were telling all kinds half-truths about me. I was not the person the gossip was making me out to be. Curtis chose to believe in me rather than the stories people were telling about me. He welcomed me and at the same time, he held me accountable. It made a big difference to me because he and Bob valued me enough to invest in me. They did not throw money at me, but instead gave me a job and a responsibility. I was determined to prove to them I was ready to change. Curtis would come by my apartment and pick me up for work each day. He became one of those good friends who was a positive influence in my life.

I can never forget people like Mr. Ulysses James. He would come by every Sunday and pick me up to go to church. Afterwards, he would buy lunch for me and we would eat together. Do you know how humbling it is for a former megastar to have someone buy him a six dollar lunch? But people like Mr. James and Curtis and Bob were people who were giving to me expecting nothing in return. That was strange. I was not sure how to handle that. Most of my life people had wanted something from me, but not these men. I had also felt like I needed to give to people too especially once I became successful. So this new experience was very humbling to me. They were good folks and were helping me become a better person.

I began coaching kids in a basketball program like the one I had grown up in. They were all amazed I had played in the NBA. The gym gave me structure. I had somewhere to go each day. Henderson was like my drug rehab. I began taking better care of myself, going to my doctor's appointments and to counseling to understand my mood swings.

Over time, I began having faith in myself again. I learned how to work with the kids and to be patient. This lesson was critical to me as a father. I had been out of my children's lives, and now I was ready to come back and be a father. I realized I could not rush in and be their dad. I knew there was a restoring process in place that would take time and I was learning to trust that process.

I started reaching out to all my children as well. DeQuan was already going to Henderson gym regularly. My daughter, London, and her mom had moved to Dallas. I went to meet her for the first time since I had held her as a baby back in Portland, which had been about 10 years earlier. I stayed with them for two months. I spent time with her, walking her to school and cooking for her. I finally got to know her.

For the first time, I met Autumn, my middle school daughter living in Cincinnati. For several years I had heard rumors about her being my daughter, but nothing had ever been confirmed. Then one day I read accusations on the internet that I was ignoring my daughter in Cincinnati. I was determined to find out because I was not about to ignore any of my children. When I discovered the truth, I wanted to meet her. Autumn and I began talking and building our relationship on the phone. She was on a dance team that had a competition in Atlanta, so I was able to meet her there for the first time. When I did, I was a bag of water.

Donjuwan was getting stronger. He was almost two years old at this point. His mom would come to Albany every weekend to see me. He was my only child I had ever seen born. Watching him struggle to live in the hospital was a stab to my conscience. I could not forget it because I felt like the whole deal was my fault. I kept thinking my drug habit had caused his mom a lot of unnecessary stress, causing her to go into labor and to give birth prematurely. I was reaping what I had sown. We were all paying for my reckless and undisciplined lifestyle. Now it was time to fix everything.

I had other reasons to reconnect with my children. I wanted their moms to know how sorry I was for how I had treated them. I wanted them to know I was doing all I could to get disability, which meant they and my children would all receive back pay. Eventually, my disability was approved. When that happened, it felt like a ton of bricks had been lifted off my back.

Chapter 31

Life was beginning to feel good again. It felt like my dreams were coming true. With my family and my own program at the gym, I felt like I had purpose. I know at the beginning, many people did not trust me because of what they had heard about Dontonio Wingfield, but their opinions no longer mattered. I kept focusing on becoming a better and stronger man.

The path for leaving my dark past was not all easy. It was an uphill battle on many fronts. I'll confess there were moments it was hard to stay away from the street life. My addictive personality would call me back. I had to fight it off.

I also had meaningful people in my life who died such as Curtis Marshall. That hurt bad. Soon after that, my two godmothers died, Mrs. Johnson and Mrs. Hudson. I cried like a baby when I lost them. I gave my college letter jacket to Mrs.

Johnson and placed it in her coffin. I gave my state championship rings to Mrs. Hudson and placed them in her coffin. They had been strong influences in my life and had meant a lot to me. Their love for me had always been unconditional. They had seen me become the leader they knew I could be. We had talked on the phone daily. They had continually reached out to me through the years. Coach Boston died during this time, too. That loss was hard because of all he had done for me in high school. If I had to name a positive male role model in my life, Coach B would be the first name I would name. Outside of basketball, he taught me a lot of things about life. About a year later, I was diagnosed with Diabetes, which eventually led to the amputation of one of my legs.

All of these painful situations encouraged me to become a better man. They also taught me to appreciate my mom more. I began to mend and strengthen my relationship with her, which brought great blessings. My dad was still living in Albany. He was still on drugs. I wouldn't go see him because when I did, I would see myself. Due to health crises, he lost both of his legs and eventually went to live in a nursing home.

What helped me through these struggles? What gave me the strength to stay strong and move forward in my new path? It was the gym and the kids. They helped me the most. I realized I could not go back. I was a leader now. Whenever I went through the ordeal with my leg amputation, my greatest desire was to get back to the gym and to work with the kids. They were my motivation. I trained so hard that I was ahead of my recovery schedule. I continued working out by lifting weights and riding a bike. I was getting stronger.

My own kids also drove me to become better. I wanted to be at their games or performances. All of them were involved in some type of team, whether it was a sport or a dance line. I was there to cheer them on. Two of my children played at Westover High School, where my jersey had been retired. It has always made me proud to watch them perform. I traveled to Cincinnati to watch D.J. play basketball. I was able to eat lunch with him and

Donovan. I loved it. Over time I became someone my children could talk to. Because of my life issues, I understood all they would experience. I also soon learned how hard it was to be a parent, especially when my children would get mad at me for being a parent, not just a friend. I was learning to trust the process, and over time, I saw things coming together. I was seeing how important it was to be in each of their lives. I was also realizing how much I had missed my own dad when I was growing up. I was becoming the very thing I had never had, a loving and present father. I was learning to not dwell on the past, but instead to make memories.

My past was a struggle, too. My conscience bothered me a great deal. I would constantly wrestle with the choices I had made. I knew I was not a bad person and that my heart was good. I was learning to have faith and to let go of my transgressions. I could not change my past; I could only go forward. And I did. I became stronger physically, mentally and spiritually.

I believe that as a result, my Albany Hawks program began to take off. I was investing in children from all over the community. It was like every kid wanted me to mentor them.

I have worked and continue to work with special people like James Nix, Chris Henderson, and Yolanda Walker, a.k.a. "Tiger." These people are individuals I know I can trust. Through time, we have developed special relationships. I was friends with James' wife, Muffin, in high school. We were more like acquaintances back then. Their daughter has been in our programs at Henderson. One day, Muffin mentioned to James that she had known me from Westover. She also added the fact that she didn't like me. So he asked her, "What has Don done to you that you don't like him?" She had no answer. Ever since, James has been like a brother from another mother to me.

Together we have mentored more than 60 kids each year through our program. I have been able to share my own experiences with them in an effort to deter a young person from traveling down a wrong path as I had done. I know the outcomes because I have been there. I have become a stable person in my community, the one where I had been raised.

I have made friends with other people who have been a tremendous help. I think of Bo, Trey, Jay, and Darrel. These men all have come from different neighborhoods and backgrounds than me, but they have wanted to help. We have learned to trust each other and our friendships are very special. These guys have brought their kids to my program trusting me to invest in them. That's been cool.

Investing in the children and teenagers of Albany has become the drive of my life. Working with other individuals, I am creating partnerships within our community such as the Pivot Foundation to help children from all backgrounds. Our goal is to provide resources for young people who have little input from adults who will invest in them and help them find their purpose. Those kinds of relationships make the difference in the life of a child. I have decided I will use the lessons I have learned from my past to change the future of kids and will encourage and influence other adults to do the same. Together we are making a

lasting impact.

The Pivot Foundation

Conclusion

When I first started thinking about telling my story with all the ups and downs, I felt my book would be about blasting the people who I felt had deserted me in my times of hardship. Or I would blame my parents, my friends, my girlfriends or my children's mothers. But my maturation was not finished. That was ten years ago. Since then I have grown and I understand more clearly what true faith is and about not giving up on yourself. My self-worth goes past my basketball successes and my life's mistakes. As I reflect on all I went through, I have come to understand how all of it gave me a strength that is undeniable. I have realized you can't be an average-minded person if you want to overcome the challenges of life.

As a young man, I felt as if I was a super hero playing basketball, and now, I have that super hero feeling again, but in a mentoring way. Although I am not using my physical abilities to perform, I get the same rush from the time I spend helping kids.

I want my own children, who are young adults now, to know their father loves them and knows that life is a journey and having faith in yourself is very important.

Words are not enough to express my gratitude to the mothers of my children. You have done a spectacular job as single moms raising some beautiful and healthy children. I honor you for being the kind of women who took seriously your role as a mom no matter what.

To my parents, I know you gave me all you had to make me the strong man I am today. I will forever love you as I want my kids to love me.

To all the kids whose lives I have touched through the Albany Hawks program and the Pivot Foundation, you have given me back my identity as a leader. Thank you! And remember, the job is not done yet!

Thanksgiving 2018 -
A Grateful Father and Grandfather!

If you are interested in having Dontonio Wingfield speak,

contact him at Albanyhawks@gmail.com or

at Facebook.com/Dontonio.wingfield

Made in the USA
Columbia, SC
17 December 2018